Listening to Children in Education

Ron Davie and David Galloway

David Fulton Publishers
London

David Fulton Publishers Ltd
2 Barbon Close, London WC1N 3JX

First published in Great Britain by
David Fulton Publishers 1996

British Library Cataloguing in Publication Data

A catalogue record for this book is available from the British Library

ISBN 1-85346-314-0

Typeset by Textype Typesetters, Cambridge
Printed in Great Britain by BPC Books and Journals Ltd, Exeter.

Contents

Acknowledgements

We are both indebted to the secretaries and technicians in the School of Education at the University of Durham for re-formatting ten different discs and putting the manuscript into a form acceptable to David Fulton. We also gratefully acknowledge the patience of our families as we worked on the book. Finally, we wish to thank warmly each of the contributors for their chapters.

Ron Davie and David Galloway
July 1995

Notes on Authors

Derrick Armstrong is a Research Fellow in the School of Education, University of Sheffield.

Marion Bennathan was formerly Principal Educational Psychologist for Avon LEA and now works independently.

Tony Charlton is a Research Fellow at Cheltenham and Gloucester College of Higher Education.

Ron Davie now works as an independent educational and child psychologist, and is visiting Professor at Oxford Brookes University and Honorary Research Fellow at University College London.

Michael Freeman is Professor of English Law at University College London and co-editor of the *International Journal of Children's Rights*.

David Galloway is Professor of Primary Education and Head of the School of Education at the University of Durham.

Teifion Griffiths is Head Teacher of St Teilo's C.W. Comprehensive School, Cardiff.

Michael Marland is Head Teacher of North Westminster Community School, London and Honorary Professor of Education at the University of Warwick

Linda Pollock is Professor of History at Tulane University, USA

Phillipa Russell is Director of the Council for Disabled Children

Disclaimers

In chapters which report the results of empirical research, all identifying details have been changed.

Part I
Setting the Scene

CHAPTER 1
The Voice of the Child in Education

Ron Davie and David Galloway

> *Headteacher Phil Buckley said that giving children a say in policy made it more difficult for them to object. 'Even at 5 years old they know they have had a voice in it'.*

The above quotation from a primary school head in Bolton may occasion some surprise. He was being interviewed by the *Times Educational Supplement* (TES, 1994) – not directly about the school's involvement of its pupils in policy-making but about the school's success in reducing playground aggression. We shall return to this initiative later. However, it illustrates well a number of aspects of this book's theme which are worth identifying straightaway.

First, giving children a say in helping shape the way their school is run can be *effective*. In this particular quotation the head singles out initially the fact that children find it more difficult to complain afterwards if they have been involved in the original decision-making. This is not the most positive of reasons but many practising teachers will warm to it!

Second, in the final sentence, the phrase 'they have had a voice in it' conveys well something which will recur throughout this book, namely, that giving children a voice in decisions tends to give them some *sense of ownership* of the final result. Third, the head reminds us that even very young children can be included in this kind of exercise.

Notice that the head makes no reference to his pupils having a *right* to be heard. He and his colleagues may feel that, too, but this is not revealed. He is here being very *practical*. This way, he says, works best.

The head makes no reference either to the very good educational reasons why the route the school has taken is good practice. The *process* involved in reaching a decision in this way is an object lesson in cooperative working which the children will also experience in different ways right across the curriculum. It therefore widens and extends the principle of cooperation from the familiar classroom groups to the wider context of the school as a whole. It can also directly be related, for example, to personal and social education, citizenship and the beginnings of self-discipline. Above all, the exercise conveys that *each pupil's views are listened to with respect*.

In this opening chapter we preview some of the themes and issues which are taken up later. The book is written predominantly for those involved in or interested in education but it would have been almost impossible to confine the book's contents narrowly to the educational field. Indeed, it would have been inappropriate to try to do so for two reasons. First, much of the recent movement in this area has been outside of education, albeit in the related fields of child law and child care. Second, as teachers know well, societal trends of any kind inevitably impact on the microcosm of school life – for better or for worse.

A growing trend

The evidence on how children were perceived and treated in earlier centuries is not easy to obtain or interpret, as Hendrick (1992) makes clear in an interesting review. Not the least of the problems is that historians have not deemed childhood to be worthy of study until quite recent years (see Chapter 2 by Linda Pollock). However, what seems clear is that in western societies at least, children have largely been seen as the chattels of their parents.Children were in a sense 'owned' by their parents who therefore had certain rights over them.

The concept – indeed the term – 'parental rights' is still with us, of course, although the present-day version tends to stress ideas of responsibility, protection and guardianship rather than ownership. Indeed, as recently as 1989 the British parliament took the step of preferring the term 'parental responsibilities' to that of 'rights' in legislation (the 1989 Children Act). Notwithstanding this, the concept of parental rights dominates most aspects of educational legislation and practice (e.g., the right of parents to remove their children from sex education lessons in school).

Victorian children, it is said, were meant to be 'seen and not heard'. However, the movement towards the protection of children from exploitation and abuse also began to gather force in the Victorian era in Britain. Inevitably, this movement encouraged the thought that children had a *right* to such protection. Interestingly, though, as Michael Freeman reminds us in Chapter 3, child protection legislation was introduced a couple of generations after legislation to protect domestic animals – 'and even then not without resistance'!

A parallel – although importantly separate – right was that adult or institutional responsibility for children should have regard to their 'best interests'. However, the ideas of children having the right to make their own choices, to exercise some autonomy, to have a 'voice' in decision-making are more modern concepts. Michael Freeman's chapter importantly highlights and analyses the implicit tension that lies between these latter ideas and the more prevalent, adult-oriented notion of acting in children's best interests.

Nevertheless, there is now increasing recognition and acceptance that children's views and perspectives need to be heard both as an ethical imperative and also as a matter of practical utility and efficacy. This chapter and indeed the rest of the book are a testament to that increasing recognition. However, in education especially – perhaps because it inevitably mirrors society – there is a long way to go before teachers as a whole accept either the probity or the value of seeking pupils' opinions or perspectives. For example, Wade and Moore (1993), in a survey of 115 primary and secondary teachers, found that less than a third of these teachers reported taking any account of the views of their pupils.

Parallels in other services

For many teachers and others in education, therefore, it may be a matter of some surprise to learn that other services concerned with children have been making rapid strides in the direction of heeding children's views for some years past.

It is always difficult to pinpoint the beginning of a trend but in social services the publication in the late 1970s by the National Children's Bureau of a slim volume called *Who Cares?* (Page and Clarke, 1977) seems to have been something of a watershed in this area. The book resulted from a modest initiative by the Bureau in bringing together young people who were in residential care to discuss their experiences. They worked in small groups under skilled group leaders and recounted onto tape how they felt about being in care. The tapes were subsequently transcribed and each group 'edited' its own account. All the accounts were fed in to the final manuscript with such professional assistance as was necessary.

As Davie (1993) has set out elsewhere, this publication clearly struck a significant chord in professional child care circles. Furthermore, it led to the formation of the National Association for Young People in Care, which developed some political influence. The title *Who Cares?* is now also the name of a regular magazine for young people in care and of a new charity which promotes their cause.

On the professional front, practice began to change quite rapidly (see Gardner, 1987). This was further accelerated by the extensive consultations which preceded the 1989 Children Act and the findings of the Cleveland Enquiry on sexual abuse (Butler-Sloss, 1988). Amongst the recommendations of this enquiry was that 'Professionals should always listen carefully to what the child has to say and take seriously what is said'.

The 1989 Children Act itself embodied the principle of listening to children. Courts henceforth, whether in care proceedings or family proceedings, had to 'have regard to...the ascertainable wishes and feelings of the child concerned (considered in the light of his age and under-standing)'.

Subsequent Guidance and Regulations made clear that this principle was not simply one for the courts to follow but for all the professionals and agencies concerned. It is thus now common practice for young people who are being looked after by local authority social services departments to be included in review meetings, together with their parents and the professionals involved. Furthermore, since Education Supervision Orders are included in this legislation, education departments are affected, too.

The criminal justice system and children

The critical difference between the law about children, discussed above, and the criminal justice system – in which children may become involved – is that the former is based on the 'welfare principle', namely, that the welfare of the child must be the court's 'paramount consideration'. In contrast, the criminal justice system in Britain is adversarial, and a child giving evidence can be subjected to the rigours of a hostile cross-examination, and the pressure, when she/he is the victim, of facing the defendant across the court.

The position until very recent years was that children's evidence was largely discounted in criminal cases. This was certainly true in respect of the younger child, on the basis of her/his assumed competence or reliability (see, e.g., Spencer, 1990). Furthermore, a hostile cross-examination is a harrowing experience for a child, especially the victim of alleged abuse, so that the police or the Crown Prosecution Service, or the child's parents, might decide not to allow the child to give evidence. In some situations, where the child was the only witness, this meant that the case could not even be brought to court, leaving the perpetrator free to offend again.

However, there has been what many regard as an astonishing revolution in the approach to children as witnesses by the normally very conservative criminal justice system (see Davie *op cit.*). This is manifest, for example, in an acceptance now that the young child may be able to give very useful evidence, in contrast to a previous dismissal of this possibility, and a readiness to look at measures to protect child witnesses from some of the rigours of courtroom procedure. These measures have included closed circuit television and screens to distance the child from the defendant and, more radically, the proposal to use video-recorded evidence from the child and then to cross-examine the child on videotape instead of at the court hearing (Pigot, 1989). Although this proposal failed by a very small margin in the House of Lords to be incorporated into legislation, it seems likely that it may be accepted in due course. In the meantime the practice of video-recording early interviews with children in abuse cases has increased. Unfortunately, but perhaps predictably, some of this use (and over-use) of the video has been undertaken without sufficient thought as to how precisely it would be utilised to best effect.

Listening to children in the health service

Like education, health has been slow to respond to current developments elsewhere. Ross (1990) was in some difficulty in finding evidence of progress in taking account of children's views in the child health field and conceded that 'there remains plenty of room for improvement'. Naish (1994) concluded that 'within health care, [children's] views are not routinely sought'. Nevertheless, she reported a number of specific initiatives as well as a major project by the Royal College of Nursing to identify and promote good practice in this area, with the support of funding from the Gulbenkian Foundation.

Further confirmation, if this were needed, of the shortcomings of the health service in this respect came at a conference on the UN Convention on the Rights of the Child, which was chaired and led by young people themselves. One young delegate with sickle cell anaemia declared:

> On visits to hospitals you get different nurses each time you go. No friendships are built up, and doctors don't listen to you. I wish hospitals could be more human. (NCB, 1994)

(It could, of course, be said that the above complaints are not exclusive to the young!)

However, one of the most significant formal decisions to clarify and endorse a young person's right to make her own decisions – given her understanding of the issues involved – emerged in the field of health. Many will recall the controversy which surrounded Victoria Gillick's appeal against her 15-year-old daughter's right to have contraceptive advice from her GP without her mother's consent. The House of Lords rejected Mrs Gillick's appeal (Gillick, 1986) in a judgement which has far-reaching implications, not yet fully thought through or tested. Again, Michael Freeman discusses this point in his chapter. Hodgkin (1994) also discusses some of the implications of 'Gillick-competency' in the context of a consideration of a young person's right to consent, or not to consent, to medical treatment.

The code of practice

We do not have to look far on the educational front for a clear indication of future trends in this area. The seminal *Code of Practice on the Identification and Assessment of Special Educational Needs* (DfE, 1994a) is, as its title indicates, concerned centrally with the 20 per cent or so of children who have significant learning difficulties. We shall return to this, too, in later chapters but for the moment it is sufficient to mark the fact that Parliament, in approving this statutory instrument, set its seal – at least for pupils with such difficulties – to the principle of involving the child, wherever possible, in decisions about provision to meet her/his special educational needs.

1993 Education Act

The absence of any reference to having regard to children's views in the educational legislation on which the Code of Practice is based is both illogical and, frankly, baffling.

First, we should recall that the Children Act some three years earlier, as we have seen above, required that due account be taken of the 'wishes and feelings' of the child in care proceedings. This means that local authority officers have to embody this principle into their work in respect of children whom they are – or may be – looking after or supervising. Part lll of the Education Act specifically deals with children who, by definition, need some kind of special care or consideration, namely, children who have special educational needs. It is even incorporated in the legislation that joint assessments by education and social services be undertaken in appropriate cases. And yet despite representations to DfE officials and to ministers, the government remained opposed to including any reference to listening to children's views in the new Education Act (see Davie, 1994).

Second, this rationale evinced only months earlier was overturned by the declaration in the Code of Practice that children's involvement in decision-making was an important matter of principle ('Children have a right to be heard'). Further, as Michael Freeman quite rightly argues, if this is an important principle in paragraph 2.35 of the Code, why is it not listed with the other principles at the beginning of the Code?

Third, the Special Educational Needs Tribunal must, like all other agencies, have regard to the Code and therefore to the principle of involving children. This is clearly reflected in the booklet for parents (SENT, 1994) which gives an answer to the question, 'Will my child have to answer questions at the hearing?' as follows:

> Your child does not have to attend the hearing. But if you *or* (our italics) your child want his or her views to be taken into account separately from your own, your child can attend the hearing and answer questions as a witness, or make a written statement.

For present purposes we shall ignore the question as to how the Tribunal can be sure whether or not the child (or, more likely, young person) wants to make her/his views known separately from the parents if s/he is not present. It suffices here to note that the Tribunal acknowledges the child's right to express a separate view and yet the legislation which established the Tribunal did not incorporate that right.

Finally, there is the UN Convention on the Rights of the Child, which is quite clear on this point. Thus, Article 12 reads:

> 1. States Parties shall assure to the child who is capable of forming his or her own views the right to express those views freely in all matters affecting the child, the view of the child being given due weight in accordance with age and maturity of the child.
>
> 2. For this purpose, the child shall in particular be provided with the opportunity to be heard in any judicial and administrative proceedings

> affecting the child, either directly or through a representative or an appropriate body, in a manner consistent with the procedural rules of natural law.

Government ministers, in debates on Part III of the Bill (concerned with special educational needs), continued to assert that the legislation did not need to include any reference to listening to the child. Their reasons for this position varied in different debates. At times they said that educational legislation, being more circumscribed than child care law, did not require such provision. At other times they said that it was a matter where individual circumstances needed to be considered.

They were challenged by the opinion of an eminent legal expert on child law, Allan Levy QC, who is used by the government in other contexts because of his expertise, that the legislation was in breach of the above article of the UN Convention (Hodgkin, 1993). Baroness Blatch for the government said, 'In the United Kingdom that provision already exists in education legislation which enables children *or their parents* (our italics) to play an active part in choices regarding their children's education.'

Allan Levy's response to the above statement was sought, and he replied:

> It is no answer, in my view, to rely upon the parent always being able to represent the child's view and position. There will, of course, be situations in which communications and representations on behalf of the child must be put quite separately. Accordingly, unless Article 12 is incorporated into the Bill, a breach of the Convention will occur.

This point was put at the Third Reading of the Bill in the Lords but Lord Henley on behalf of the government merely restated what Baroness Blatch had said earlier.

Evidence of progress on the educational front

Notwithstanding this intransigence by the government at the legislative stage, it does appear that some light shone through in the period between the passing of the Bill and the drafting of the Code of Practice. Ministers at the Department for Education were now apparently prepared to accept (para.2.35) not only that listening to children had practical benefits but that 'children have a right to be heard'.

The implementation of the Code from September 1994 will have focused schools' attention on this principle, and a number of local authorities and others have subsequently produced guidance or training packs on this aspect of the Code (e.g., Morton, 1994).

However, the evidence on the extent to which schools in general accept or apply the principle of heeding children's views seems to be equivocal. For example, Gersch (in press) is optimistic about current progress and trends in this respect. He surveyed 87 schools and colleges in a London borough and found that, 'The overwhelming majority of respondents indicated that pupil involvement should be encouraged and also felt that to some extent it was being encouraged in their institutions'. However, his response rate, although quite good by the normal standards of such surveys, was only around 40 per cent and the views of the overwhelming majority of his respondents may have represented a minority position if the views or practices of all the institutions were known.

A less optimistic note than Gersh's is indicated by research carried out by Wade and Moore (1993), as we saw earlier. They found in a survey of mainstream teachers that less than a third said that they took account of the views of their pupils. A number of the teachers even commented that they regarded this as time-consuming and of little value.

The value of listening to children in schools

The evidence on the present position in schools is therefore not entirely clear but seems to leave no room for complacency on the part of those who believe that pupil involvement in its various forms is both an important principle as well as an effective practice.

However, the evidence on this latter point is growing and, coming as it does from a variety of sources and contexts, appears increasingly convincing. As long ago as 1984, Davie and his colleagues reported that senior managers from mainstream secondary schools on a two-year INSET course were extremely impressed by the common sense and insight of their pupils when these were asked about aspects of school life. Many of the teachers were initially sceptical about the value of consulting their pupils, it being seen as somewhat analogous to consorting with the enemy! However, when the teachers were required by the course to find some way of doing this – for example, by questionnaire or by discussing with small groups – the teachers were often astounded by the balanced views which emerged.

One of the headteachers on the course chose to carry out this exercise with a small (but 'difficult') class over several weeks, using a questionnaire that he and the pupils devised together. This very experienced headteacher reported later not only that the information produced was valuable but that his relationship with that class had been 'transformed' by the experience.

The course as a whole was judged to be very successful in producing change in the schools – and sustaining it over time. The evaluation of the course (Davie *et al.*, 1984) highlighted a number of aspects which were responsible for this. Amongst them was the structured experience of consulting pupils, which for most of the course members and their schools was a new departure. There seemed to be something about this particular experience which struck home and was a lesson which, once learnt, was never forgotten.

Vulliamy and Webb (1991) reached a somewhat similar conclusion in examining factors which facilitated the change process in the context of school-based research enquiries undertaken by teachers on award-bearing training courses. Interestingly, the authors found that over half of these enquiries (N=127) had obtained data from pupils. The authors report that 'a major effect of the research on the practice of course members was in their changed attitudes towards their pupils and the value they came to ascribe to their views'.

One of the teachers involved, a deputy head, had used his pupils' experiences of and opinions about the transfer from primary to secondary schooling in his study of that process. He later commented in interview,

> It's changed our way of teaching quite a bit. You go through a kind of de-skilling phase when you think, well, what I was doing before was totally wrong, or whatever...But it certainly made me think a lot more of why and how.

This finding that listening to children may be a powerful and enduring learning experience for teachers may also have been picked up by Francis (1993) in the context of the initial training of teachers. She set out to encourage her trainees to listen to 'learners' voices' and to obtain 'a genuine view of learners as social and personal selves'. Francis felt that,

> teachers who are not aware of the importance of learners' understandings of and feelings about the nature and significance of learning tasks are unlikely to see that there may be a fundamental lack of agreement between their own and their students' conceptions.

Francis found that when her trainee teachers put this 'listening' approach into practice, their perspectives on their pupils changed and the pupils' learning improved. Francis cautions that she has no long-term evidence on the extent to which the teachers maintained these new perspectives, although in incidental feedback 'some later reported that they had'.

Other experiences of involving pupils

The evidence set out above has come largely from academics, or from research studies. Tony Charlton's chapter (Chapter 4) adds greatly to the sum total of evidence of this nature. However, there will be those readers who, for whatever reason, will place more reliance on the direct testimony and experience of 'hands on' professionals whose responsibilities resume every Monday morning of term time. Of course, such a distinction drawn between academics, researchers and practitioners is less and less valid, for much research draws on the perspectives of such practitioners and some of it, as we have seen, is actually carried out by them.

Thus, Marion Bennathan's chapter (Chapter 7) draws directly on the experience of schools which have adopted and assimilated the philosophy of listening to and consulting their pupils, and it makes fascinating reading. However, for those (perhaps of a sceptical persuasion) who feel the need to read the words of wisdom straight from the senior management team, two of the chapters in our book are written by serving heads who have risen to the very top of their profession and write with great conviction from this platform of successful experience.

It seems clear, too, that the experiment at the Bolton primary school referred to at the beginning of this chapter was seminal not only for the headteacher and his colleagues but also for their pupils and the parents. The focus of the initiative was on various aspects of discipline, including playground behaviour and bullying. In addition, it stretched to 'codes of conduct' drawn up by each year group on, for example, classroom tidiness, looking after equipment, general courtesy towards others and on rewards and punishments. In this latter connection, the headteacher comments that,

> The children came up with fairly severe ideas for retribution which have been effective, such as removal of privileges and not using the computer. The parents have also been very supportive and want to know if their child is misbehaving.

One local authority which seems to be convinced that children are making choices and which is seeking to making those choices better informed is the London Borough of Hammersmith and Fulham. They have produced a brochure for Year 6 pupils which sets out to help them in the decision about which secondary school to choose. This publication ('Making Your Mind Up') is based on the assumption, (confirmed by research findings from Newcastle University) that 'most children rather than their parents choose their secondary school' (TES, 1992).

Some dangers in involving pupils in decision-making

As always, if one is seeking a sensible answer to a problem, one needs to pose the right question. Derrick Armstrong and David Galloway in Chapter 8 offer a timely reminder about one kind of danger. This starts with the by-now familiar trap of using what is sometimes called a 'deficit model' in approaching a situation where a child has difficulties. However, as Armstrong and Galloway point out, the step of involving the child may increase this danger.

The essence of the deficit model is the assumption that the problem is somehow located in the child. It is he/she who has the difficulty, so that 'remedial' action is focused upon dealing with him/her. However, a great deal of research in the past 20 years or so has highlighted the differences between schools (with similar intakes) in the extent and nature of the problems which their pupils display. This has prompted the more or less common sense conclusion that schools can make a difference for the worse as well as for the better. Therefore, a particular problem which appears to be a child's may mostly be a reflection of an unsatisfactory situation within the school.

Unless this possibility is always borne in mind, there is the danger that an attempt to involve the child will start with the implicit question, 'Why are *you* a problem?' rather than the more neutral 'How has this problem arisen?' The added danger therefore in involving the child in such a situation is that if the dialogue were to start from the wrong premise and the child were to accept this, the deficit model would be powerfully reinforced.

Another danger which can arise from involving children in decision-making is that of encouraging false expectations on the child's part. This can be seen at its most stark perhaps in the disclosure by a child to a teacher of sexual abuse. The involvement of a child in these situations must never be accompanied by an assurance of confidentiality, nor that the course of subsequent events can follow the 'wishes and feelings' of the child. Many children who disclose this problem wish the abuse to stop but for the family otherwise to be unaffected. In most circumstances this outcome is not possible and unless the initial disclosure and subsequent counselling are carefully and skilfully handled, the child may feel let down, even betrayed.

Such situations are fortunately rare, at least for most teachers, but they do highlight the more general difficulty of eliciting a child's view without encouraging her/him to believe that this view will prevail or that it is necessarily valid. The central feature of involving children in decisions is that their views are being taken seriously and are being accorded due weight. This, of course, begs the question as to what 'due weight' should be given and who is to decide this. Some of these issues are further discussed by Michael Freeman.

Lessons from implementing the 1989 Children Act

As we have seen earlier, the 1989 Children Act clearly embodied the principle of having regard to the 'ascertainable wishes and feelings' of the child. Further, even before the legislation was introduced, the practice of involving children – for example, those who are being 'looked after' by a local authority – in their own annual reviews was relatively commonplace. However, as every teacher will know in respect of the much vaunted 'partnership with parents', it is possible for such developments to be little more than slogans.

Smith (in press) looks at how social services departments have been implementing the principle of listening to children, since the 1989 Act. In the age-old terminology of countless school reports, Smith's implicit verdict on his colleagues is: 'could do better':

> Thus, whilst there is evidence of good practice in ascertaining the wishes and feelings of children in, for example, some residential homes and by many guardians *ad litem*, the overall picture is patchy and illustrates the need for social workers to pay greater attention to consulting with children.

In addition, of course, there has been the predictable reaction from professionals who fear that their control of situations has been loosened. Thus, for example, Wolkind (1993), a child psychiatrist who declares that he was 'swept up in the wave of enthusiasm for the changes in the law', was expressing fears a year later that 'the interests of children in Britain may have been put back many years by the implementation of the Act'. On the question of listening to children he cites the case of a difficult 10-year-old who 'told us confidently in his interview that he had nothing to say to us, as he had instructed his solicitor to oppose the interim care order'. This situation was no doubt very annoying for the clinical team and could have been 'worsening this boy's difficulties'. However, to throw such doubt on the value of one of the most comprehensively researched pieces of social legislation in this century on the basis of a number of case histories gathered over one year by one clinician seems overreactive.

Nevertheless, it remains a truism that if one gives a group of people a new power, especially if they have been deprived of it before, some of these people will abuse it, especially in the early stages of the change process. Such abuse will inevitably provoke those who have experienced a corresponding loss of power to declare that the end of the world is nigh and that they predicted, or suspected, such a cataclysmic outcome. In this case, the new power is a modest one for children, namely, the right to have adults listen to their perspective and to have this taken seriously. However, even such modest advances can, it seems, threaten some adult bastions. Hopefully, though, most professionals, whether in education, health or child care, will see the benefits – not to mention the probity – of listening to children's perspectives. Children may sometimes be naive or immature in this; at times they may be manipulative; they may sometimes lie, too. However, we need no research evidence to convince us that children have no monopoly of these characteristics.

Part II
The Historical and Legal Background

CHAPTER 2

Teacher-Pupil Relations in Eighteenth and Nineteenth Century Britain

Linda A. Pollock

The history of education has begun to broaden its scope beyond a narrative account of the increasing extent of educational provision, and/or an analysis of literacy levels. By now we are well informed about such issues as the establishment of schools, attendance records, the extension of working-class education, and the prevalence of literacy in the past. More recent work has begun to examine schools within the context of their culture, revising in the process notions of working-class indifference to education (Gardner, 1984; Laqueur, 1976). However, we still know little about the world within the school (an exception being Roach, 1986); and in particular the nature of the teacher-pupil relationship. Moreover, to deal with this topic properly, we must also examine the governess/tutor-pupil relationship, especially with reference to the experience of girls.

This chapter will examine relations between teachers and pupils at home and at school in the working, middle and upper classes prior to the education act of 1870. The picture is not as bleak as some authors have suggested. Many children were happy at school. Nevertheless, the emphasis was on children listening to adults, not the other way round. Although the state and working-class parents were often in conflict over the aims of education, both saw it in strictly instrumental terms. Schooling was a process for socialising the young, not for listening to them. We will begin with a brief overview of the nature of education in the eighteenth and nineteenth centuries, followed by an examination of what parents, teachers and the state expected of education and conclude with an analysis of the experience of pupils at school.

The nature of education in the eighteenth and nineteenth century

The concept of consistent, continuous, lengthy association between teacher and pupil is a modern notion born of the repercussions from compulsory schooling. Prior to 1870, education was voluntary and often, particularly for the poorer ranks, erratic. Children alternated between work, home and school, and they changed schools often. A survey of educational provision reveals that by the eighteenth century many young people would have the chance of some education. However, education for most children was sporadic and discontinuous (Rule, 1992; 145–7). Only a very few working-class children received a formal education before 1780, usually by attending charity schools (Goldstrom, 1972; 11). Until the last decades of the eighteenth century, literacy levels for adult males were about 30–40 per cent. These rates were much higher for artisans and shopkeepers; and much lower for women (Rule, 1992; 140).

Nevertheless, by the 1850s many children did at least have contact with the world of education and learning through the Sunday School system. It is estimated that there were about 100,000 Sunday pupils by 1800. Fifty years later, there were about 3,000 charity schools and Sunday Schools with over two million children enrolled in them. State education was not the only option available. There were twice as many private as state schools with one third of all pupils enrolled in private schools (Hopkins, 1994; ch. 5). Of the 123,000 children attending school in five Midlands cities in the 1830s, some 50,000 were pupils at dame schools (Gosden, 1969; 8).

Notwithstanding the improvements in access to education by the nineteenth century, the facilities supplied were not always conducive to learning. The rooms were often stuffy and poorly lit (Hurt, 1971; 69, 75–6). Schools until well into the nineteenth century were usually one room, with the teacher at the desk, most children on benches, and a few learning to write at desks. More elite institutions would have several classrooms and more than one master. But even in a public school like Eton, all classes were crammed into one room (Gathorne-Hardy, 1977). Classes were often large, invariably noisy and the school day about six hours long, at times longer. Joseph Ashby, recalling his infant school in 1860s, remembers how noisy it was, and how tedious the reading lessons were while waiting for slower pupils to complete their section (Gosden, 1969; 40–41).

Teaching methods until late in the eighteenth century, and for the lower classes even beyond, were designed not to encourage critical and independent thinking but to instil a fixed set of ideas and facts into pupils:

'The aim was not to expand imaginative understanding but to guide the mind along certain set paths ... orthodoxy was prized much more than originality' (Houston, 1988; 56). Thus memorising material played a large role; in fact in most elementary schools this was the only means of learning offered to children. Constant repetition, it was believed, would instil the habits of learning. Reading was taught by first memorising the alphabet, then the letters out of order, then the child learnt to identify syllables, whole words, and finally phrases. Learning to write was also primarily a task of copying rather than creating (Houston, 1988; ch. 2; Hughes, 1993; 75).

It was not necessary to attend school, however, to receive some education. The 1851 census revealed that 21,000 women were employed as governesses, rising to almost 25,000 ten years later (Horn, 1989; 333). The term 'governess' could refer to a woman who taught in a school, a woman who lived at home and travelled to her employer's house to teach, or a woman who lived in her employer's home and taught the children and served as a companion to them. A governess could expect to receive a low salary and although she was housed and fed, she was expected to pay for laundry, travel and medical care and to maintain an appropriate standard of dress. Moreover the hours were long since she was usually required to supervise children constantly in addition to lesson hours (Peterson, 1973; 4, 5, 7, 12).

Employers certainly wished to hire a gentlewoman but a lady was increasingly being defined as a person of leisure. Therefore a governess, as an employed lady, embodied in her person a contradiction of the very values she was meant to fulfil. The result was a situation of conflict and incongruity, not an ideal circumstance for the interactive acquisition of knowledge (Peterson, 1973; Hughes, 1993).

What parents, teachers and the state expected of education

The education of elite men had long been regarded as a necessity, whereas the education of girls and, even more, of the working-classes, struggled to gain acceptance. Education existed not to liberate minds but to preserve the distinctions of society, of status and gender. Schools were organised around cultural models of what was appropriate. The poor were to be trained to be orderly, productive members of society. Hence in the Blue- and Grey-Coat charity schools in eighteenth-century York, five hours a day were to be spent on spinning and weaving, with reading, writing and the rules of arithmetic thrown in only as a 'relief from more painful tasks' (Houston, 1988; 14, 22). By the late 1830s, those who believed that education could be used as a means of preserving social order, as opposed to those who thought that the working classes would cease to labour if they were educated, had won the day. But if schooling were to be an instrument of conformity, this meant that the type of education supplied had to be carefully regulated. The working classes who attended the state-run schools were plunged into a different cultural world in which the teachers' explicit agenda was to reform their behaviour; in fact, to inoculate them against 'those habits of sloth, debauchery and irreligion', which were thought of as increasingly characteristic of the lower orders (Rule, 1992; 144). Education in the main was designed to condition the poor for their humble positions in life as servants and labourers (Goldstrom, 1972; 11).

The state's vision of the appropriate education of the working classes was not consistent with working class aims. Schooling to them was not necessarily a course of discipline but a means of acquiring such skills as reading, writing, arithmetic, sewing and knitting, preferably quickly, as a preparation for earning a living. Their attitude was shaped by a keen awareness of the lack of resources like time and money. This meant that patterns of school attendance for the poor were intermittent rather then regular (Gardner, 1984; 74). Schooling was even more irregular for girls since daughters were more likely to be kept home than their brothers to mind the baby and help with other domestic tasks (Purvis, 1989; 76).

The state wanted to break working-class attachment to private schooling, attributing their preference for it over the public elementary schools to working class ignorance. The perspective of the working classes, however, was entirely rational. They preferred the flexibility of the private schools and that the time spent there was concentrated on basic skills without the resented and time-consuming element of moral instruction which formed an integral part of the public school's curriculum. The private teachers did not insist on regular attendance nor perfect cleanliness. Parents and teachers were often drawn from the same cultural milieu and there could be close relationships between them. The customers appear satisfied with the education offered at the small private schools. Joseph Kenworthy, a 12-year-old factory worker from Birmingham, for example, was described as follows:'Can read and write a little. Went to Mr Raysbeck's day school. Is taught to read, write, spell and sum. Thinks he gets on pretty well' (Gardner, 1984; 28–9, 88, 95–6).

The middle and upper classes also had their own expectations of schooling. That schools were expected to convey academic superiority is clear. Daniel Sandford, in a letter to his son at boarding school in 1813, assured him that attending school was an advantage: 'My constant employment would have prevented me from attending to you, and without daily attention, at this critical period, you could make no progress in Greek' (Sandford, 1830; vol. 1, 259). However, unlike those lower down the social scale, the more affluent sections of society also sought the moral training educational establishments were meant to provide. Frances, Lady Shelley, intended to send her second son to Eton in 1820 in order to strengthen his character:

> Frederick is a shy, amiable, industrious boy, not wanting in abilities, but a little cowed – if you know what I mean – by the superiority of his elder brother, which I think a year at Eton will remove; and the independence he will acquire there will be of use to him before he goes to sea (Shelley, 1912; vol. 2, 102).

John and Kate Russell encountered many problems trying to control their unruly son Frank. They were planning to send him to school in 1872 because, as John Russell explained:

> Obedience is not the most important; but surely they must be prevented from doing things which injure themselves or others and be taught that some little deference is due to others' wishes instead of requiring every body to defer to theirs. Public schools are of immense value in this way and for some I think almost indispensable (Russell, 1966; vol. 2, 511).

Even for the middle classes, educational provision could lack continuity as children alternated between home and school tuition as well as changing schools. John Townsend, born in 1757, at first attended a dames school, then went to two different boy's schools but made little progress. Finally, his mother in 1774 'by means of one of his father's more wealthy brothers, procured him a presentation to Christ's Hospital' and he was sent there from 1774 to 1779 (Townsend, 1828; 5). Edward Pease, born in 1767, was sent to various schools until 11, but his parents did not consider his time well spent and from the age of 12 to 14, he attended a boarding school with a more rigorous academic programme (Pease, 1907). Parents sought specific advantages, usually only some of which could be met by any one school, and were prepared to change schools as often as was necessary in order to satisfy all their requirements.

Public schools aimed to mould the character of middle-class boys and prepare them for success in professional and public life; middle-class girls were educated to be potential wives and mothers who would be supported economically. Hence they were taught the type of ornamental knowledge that would be useful in attracting a husband (Jordan, 1991;

Purvis, 1989). Schooling for girls could be sought for the academic opportunity it provided. The Reverend John Mill, for example, in 1768 was delighted he had his eldest daughter Nell, aged about 12,

> settled with the Miss Scots, a minister's daughter of good reputation, to teach her to make her own clothes, at least, and see more of the world, as she had got already what this country [Lerwick] afforded as to sewing and working of stockings, writing, arithmetic, dancing, church music and co (Mill, 1889; 31).

It was also sought for the discipline it imposed. Priscilla Johnston, when asked her opinion on school for girls in 1849, stated 'There is nothing like, in my judgment, the regularity, discipline, self-denial, and entirely new and educational atmosphere of a school'. She regarded her experience at school as entirely beneficial:

> 'I gained most important advantages in tone of education as well as in actual acquirement; I gained some ease of manner, and that sort of undefined enlargement which there is in familiar intercourse with persons of a new sort; but above all, I think I gained religious decision.

That is, the having to decide herself what was right and what was wrong was 'one of the most important processes I ever went through' (Johnston, 1862; 186). Charlotte Papendiek at the beginning of the nineteenth century was explicit about what she hoped to achieve for her daughters:

> My desire was that my girls should remain as day scholars with Mrs Roach, where they would continue under my guidance, and I could watch their daily progress, knowing at the same time that they were with a women of strict principle if not altogether of the ornamental manner of good breeding (Broughton, 1887; vol. 2, 279).

Schools did not exist to 'listen' to their young clients; they were there to help mould the young into shape.

Teachers in private schools for girls were animated by different values from the headmistresses of the public schools of the late nineteenth century. Like governesses, women who kept private schools were members of that peculiar social category – impecunious ladies obliged to work for pay. The family was the model for the small private school: small, exclusive and run on similar lines to a private home. The content of the education they gave was in keeping with the values of the ladies who taught and reflected their leisured ideal. The accomplishments which dominated the curriculum were also the most profitable subjects to teach: core subjects of music and French, supplemented with English, history, geography, arithmetic, needlework, religion, and at times drawing, dancing, piano, German and science (Pedersen, 1975; 138–46).

Anna Braithwaite, for instance, who was born in 1788, was sent to boarding school at the age of 10 and studied history, geography, French, Italian and English grammar (Braithwaite, 1905; 20).

The range of subjects offered was large and the teachers were not specialised. It was more important for the women to have principles, refinement and for them to act as models of elegance and moral rectitude for pupils rather than to transmit expert knowledge. Their accomplishments were often more valued for the indication they gave that the woman in question was well-born than for any promise they held of her effectiveness as an educator (Pedersen, 1975; 138–46). Similar principles were applied to the selection of governesses if it was intended that girls be educated at home. Lady Stanley in 1843 desired a governess for her granddaughters who would hopefully 'improve their minds', but even more importantly would be of impeccable breeding since 'the *manners* of a gentlewoman are *essential* especially as they generally though not always prove the *mind* of one besides' (Mitford, 1938; 59).

The organising principle of education in this period was not that of listening to children but that of training them for their future roles in life, no matter how resistant the individual child might be. Lessons were imparted and as the child learnt them their opinions were not sought nor welcomed. These views meant that although a child's temperament could be taken into account, this was only so far as was necessary to find the best way to ensure the internalisation of society's norms:

> ...the tutor and attendant should discover, by imperceptible means, the inclinations and tastes of each pupil, directing their pastimes into such channels as may tend to divert evil propensities, and give encouragement to rational pleasures and pursuits. This is the great secret and difficulty of education, and makes it necessary that we should exercise great judgment in our selection of those to whose care we entrust the development of our children's minds (Broughton, 1887; vol 1, 94–5).

Far from paying attention to children, the child was meant to please the teacher. As Reginald Heber advised his son Richard at school in London in 1783:

> You will I trust, my dear, endeavour to deserve the continuance of your worthy tutor's favour and good opinion and I am sure you will be very happy and improve greatly under his care. A ready obedience to his commands, diligent attention to his instructions, and assiduous application to your business will infallibly ensure you the applause, love, and affection of your master. Than which nothing in this life can afford greater satisfaction to me, and the rest of your friends (Heber mss; 7).

Or, as John Parker warned his 9-year-old son Christopher, sent to school in 1863,

> You may be quite sure that nothing will make school happy so much as trying to do all things well, and trying as much as possible to please Mr Wickham, [headmaster] and this I hope you will do to the utmost of your power (Parker, 1964; 241).

In the nineteenth century, children were taught to be obedient to parents, and to teachers. Such maxims as 'When you go to school, your teachers take the place of your parents. ... They ought therefore to be obeyed accordingly' or 'A good scholar is known by his obedience to the rules of the school, and to the directions of his teachers,' were imparted early. One of the main tasks of the public and charity schools was to teach the poor to obey. The young were trained to work hard, and, moreover, to view the performance of their duty as their chiefest pleasure (Walvin, 1982; 104, 105).

Children's experience of school

The timetable for school and home education was usually long and heavily structured, reflecting the essentially instrumental aims of education. The curriculum, teaching methods, the organisation of the school day and the discipline system all emphasised the importance of children adapting to adult requirements. Childhood was a precious learning time of life and should not be wasted. Rather, effort should be expended consistently in acquiring skills for the future. The idea that children should have a say in their own education is a peculiarly twentieth century one, and late twentieth century at that. Sydney Owenson in the 1790s was sent to what was reputed to have been the best school in Ireland and she herself regarded the education she received there as very good. The girls rose at 6 a.m. in summer and 7 a.m. in winter. On rising, weather permitting, they bathed in the sea. This was followed by prayers, English lessons, grammar and geography – all before breakfast. After a meal of bread and milk, there was play in the gardens, and more studies between 12 noon to 3 p.m. At 3.30, the pupils ate dinner and enjoyed more play until supper at 7. Homework was completed in the evening and finally, at 9 p.m., prayers were said and the pupils retired to bed. During the week, Sydney had extra private masters for music and dancing (Owenson, 1863; 69).

At home, the schedule for boys and girls was equally rigorous, if not more so. Marjory Fleming at the age of 8 was under the tuition of her cousin Isabella. Her daily schedule consisted of: from 7 in the morning until 8 dancing, then bible reading; then play until 10. From 10 until 11 she studied music; from 11 to 12 writing and accounts, and from 12 to 1 she sewed. She was then permitted free play until dinner after which she learnt grammar and then worked until 5 p.m. In the evening from 7 to 8, Marjory knitted. She was quite content with her daily routine, apart from multiplication which she regarded as a 'horrible and wretched plague ... the most devilish thing is 8 times 8 and 7 times 7. It is what nature itself can't endure' (Fleming, 1934; 46, 66).

Frank Dryden, tutored by Mr Denison, had a similarly austere regime (see Table 2.1).

Table 2.1 Frank Dryden, tutored by Mr Denison in the early nineteenth century, adhered to an austere scholarly regime

	Before Breakfast 7 to 9	After from 10 to 11		After dinner from 4 to 6	
Monday	Greek Homer	Mathematics	French History	Cicero	Latin verse
Tuesday	Greek prose	Logic	French History	Virgil	Rhetoric
Wednesday	Greek Homer	Mathematics	French History	Cicero	Latin verse
Thursday	Greek prose	Logic	French History	Virgil	Rhetoric
Friday	Greek Homer	Mathematics	French History	Cicero	Latin verse
Saturday	Greek prose	Logic	French History	Virgil	Rhetoric

> Mr. Denison to give Frank a theme alternately in Latin and English from history to compose of an evening, beginning first with narration and thus progressively to the higher species of composition to finish it for Mr Denison's examination in the morning (Dryden mss; 283).

These schedules expected a great deal of young people, especially in terms of intellectual stamina, patience and concentration.

Many parents and children were fully satisfied with the teachers they had hired. William Lucas, the father of nine children, 15 years old and younger, in 1847 wrote: 'We find William Dawson a very efficient and satisfactory tutor and it is pleasant to see that the children respect and like him very much' (Lucas, 1934; 390). Annie de Rothschild, aged 13, was delighted with her Hebrew tutor in 1858: 'It is extraordinary how the little Doctor teaches, how he tells you a world of knowledge with every date'. This tutor also shared in his charge's pastimes:

> The little Doctor remarkably chatty; have a race with him, shame to me he wins. All my boots fault! Mrs Fowler gives us very good wine; return, have another race. Alas he won. Then we had a jumping match over a ditch. At last very merry we came home (Cohen, 1935; 80, 81).

Pupils, attending schools, however, could be more unfortunate. William Harvey was bewildered by his first exposure to Latin and the teacher offered no aid:

> I went down in the afternoon twice a week to a school in the village conducted by a Mr Wilson. It was not a good school, and Mr Wilson, though never actually the worse for drink, was obviously not the better for his addiction to it. When I first presented myself I was given a copy of Abbott's *Via Latina*, open at the first conjugation, which I was told to learn. I had no idea what was meant by a tense or a mood. The perfect tense to my mind seemed anything but perfect, and the pluperfect, which sounded as if it ought to be very good, was worse than bad. I tried to concentrate my mind on loving (present participle) and those things which Romans considered meet to be loved (Harvey, 1936; 98-9).

However, William did learn. His progress was slow but after some time he could decline tables and construct simple sentences.

Discipline is the feature of schools in the past which has probably received the most attention. Conventional wisdom has it that corporal punishment was an integral part of education in previous centuries. Punishments were harsh for both the working class and the elite. For the working classes, school was an alien, threatening place, replete with canes, severe punishment and an unrelenting stress on the necessity of obedience (Hopkins, 1994; 140). The public school world was one of violence, bullying and floggings (Gathorne-Hardy, 1977). In the report of the council of education prepared in 1845, it was found that out of 163 schools examined, 145 relied on corporal punishment (Gosden, 1969; 18). This evidence is borne out by more personal testimony. William Steadman, born in 1764 to poor parents, was sent to a dame school where the schoolmistress rapped the heads of her pupils with a long stick (Steadman, 1838; 5). Anthony Cooper, the seventh Earl of Shaftesbury, attended at the age of 7 in 1808 a school which he later described as, 'dreadful' with no proper supervision or food, and with cruel punishments, as well as bullying. In his old age, he commented, 'The memory of that place makes me shudder; it is repulsive to me even now.

I think there never was such a wicked school before or since. The place was bad, wicked, filthy; and the treatment was starvation and cruelty'. But at the age of 12 he was sent to Harrow and loved it (Cooper, 1886; vol. 1, 39, 41). John Epps, born in 1806, attended a boarding school at the age of 9 in which a great deal of physical punishment was administered:

> In the holidays, in order to prepare my hands for the stripes they were to receive during the next half-year, I every day gave myself twenty stripes on the hands with a switch. Also having heard that our gardener had acquired a thick skin by the use of the spade, I took to digging hard in my father's garden. By these means, I gained such stoical firmness that, on going back to school, when ordered *to put out my hand* for strokes of the cane, I held it with as much firmness as did Mutius Scaevola *his* in the flame before King Parsenna (Epps, 1875; 45).

Some masters clearly enjoyed inflicting pain:

> At this school there were several masters. I more generally received my punishment from a reverend gentleman. This was the principal, but he was a man I never could like. I fear he was a selfish man; and certainly he evinced a spiteful disposition. But he is gone, and I hope to heaven. When he saw me hold out my hand with firmness, he would raise his arm the higher, and would bring down his cane with the additional force imparted by anger. When he had exhausted his venom without being able to move me, he was obliged to say, 'Go to your seat, sir'. This master used to have the cobbler's cord wound round the end of his cane, so that the poor schoolboy might suffer more (Epps, 1875; 46).

John Epps did not think this was an effective disciplinary regime: the punishments were too frequent, too severe and too often for trifling faults. He did not learn much at school, he and all the other boys learnt like parrots, and were constantly longing for home. Thomas Acland, born in 1809, spent his seventh to twelfth years at a private school under a severe master. Acland was whipped often for small offences like arrears in work, or being last down in the morning; he felt as though he were being crushed (Acland, 1902). James Gaskell went to Eton in 1824 and was very unhappy at first, particularly with the bullying and with corporal discipline.

> He [a master] first flogged one of the colleges, then called for me. I begged him to give me my first fault. He answered that I had committed an error very early. I scarcely refrain from tears, but did.

James did settle down and seemed happier for the rest of his stay (Gaskell, 1883; 3).

In the public and private schools there was a pronounced tendency to cane boys, but not girls (Gosden, 1969; 43). This does not mean, however, that the treatment meted out to girls was necessarily more lenient. Frances, Lady Shelley, born in 1787, went to school at the age of 8:

> Marks of approbation and of disgrace, were pinned on our frocks. I seem to have been always in disgrace! I was wilful, headstrong, and determined to have my own way. The youngest sister of Miss Dutton, who kept the school, took me in charge, but in spite of violence and smacking, she could not subdue me (Shelley, 1912; vol. 1, 5).

Elizabeth Sewell, born in 1815, was sent to day school with her sisters at a young age. She did not like school but was too afraid of the teacher to complain. A strict discipline was applied to all: no talking in class; if a pupil made three mistakes in a lesson – and a hesitation counted as a mistake – she had to do another lesson; offenders had to stand in front of the class wearing a mark of disgrace such as brown paper ass's ears. Elizabeth once told a lie and was punished by being forced to wear the liar's gown and tongue, feeling very ashamed and disgraced. Elizabeth was sent to boarding school at the age of 13 and the strict regime there made her nervous and anxious (Sewell, 1907; 4, 9, 10).

The discipline of a governess could also be severe. Melesina Trench, born 1768, whose parents were both dead by 1772, was reared by her paternal grandfather from the age of 4 to 6. There she had a governess whom she hated and feared: 'I shall not dwell on the cruelties I suffered, possibly from the best intentions' (Trench, 1862, 4). Mary Haldane, born in 1825, recollected of her governess:

> She was a very strict disciplinarian, and we were vigorously punished when we infringed the laws of the schoolroom .... The system of the day was to administer corporal punishment. We, or rather I, as my sister escaped from having had scarlet fever and being pronounced delicate, were shut up for a day at a time and fed only on bread and water .... While with Miss Taylor our feet were placed in the stocks during lesson time, and we held a back board behind our backs, being seated on a narrow seat that only just held us (Haldane, 1925; 43, 44, 45).

The inflexibility of such regimes was difficult to endure. However, although some children could experience harsh discipline in the course of their education, in practice severe punishment was frowned upon by parents and authorities (Houston, 1988; 62; Pollock, 1983; chp. 5). Louisa Hardy, in 1820, was upset when her daughter's governess became severe and 'beat little Mary most cruelly' (Gore, 1935; 71). John Bright, born in 1811, attended a school reputed to supply a good training for Quakers. Unfortunately, John found the routine brutal and the punishments 'barbaric'. He particularly hated the cold baths: 'I cannot describe the terror which seized and afflicted me of the mornings when I had to undergo the inevitable plunge'. John's sufferings induced his father to investigate other schools and 'he placed before the Committee of Management facts to prove that a thorough reform was needed' (Bright, 1930; 6, 7).

Lady Charlotte Guest was unhappy at the prospect of sending her sons to Eton in 1845 but felt unable to stop it:

> When I thought of all the sorrow and temptation my poor boys would have to go through in that place I quite shuddered and prayed that assistance might be granted them from above. It seems a sad prospect, but everybody says it is the only way to bring up boys; and what is to be done! How can I a poor weak woman, judge against all the world? (Guest, 1950; 164).

Sydney Smith was similarly reluctant about his son Douglas, almost 15 in 1820, going to school for the first time. Douglas was to attend Westminster. Smith had made inquiries into several schools for Douglas and was well aware of the system:

> Douglas is gone to school; not with a light heart, for the first year of Westminster in college is severe:– an intense system of tyranny, of which the English are very fond, and think it fits a boy for the world; but the world, bad as it is, has nothing half so bad (Smith, 1953; vol. 1, 345).

The impotence of the wealthier ranks is in striking contrast to the behaviour of the working classes who would personally complain to teachers if one of their children was harshly punished (Gardner, 1984; 104).

The history of discipline in education is a dismal tale but it is not completely black. Not all schools were harsh; not all pupils endured severe punishments even at those places with strict regimes; and not all teachers were unpleasant (Hughes, 1993; 59; Gardner, 1984; 214). Frances Shelley, discussed above, experienced difficulties with one teacher, but had fond memories of another: 'the elder sister, a delicate gentle creature, took me under her care, and I shall never cease to remember her kindness, her judicious management, and the strong affection which she inspired' (Shelley, 1912; vol. 1, 5). Many diarists have commented on how much they enjoyed their school experience.

John Pollen went to Eton in 1833 and had nothing but delightful memories of it despite the image of brutality the establishment possessed

(Pollen, 1912). Henry Alford in 1824 went to grammar school and was happy there (Alford, 1873). Margaret Jeune described her son Fritz's contentment with his boarding school in 1859: 'He is a contented, happy-tempered child – likes his school, his masters, food, etc.' (Jeune, 1932; 79). The diary of the schoolboy Thomas Whitwell, covering the period 1827–8, contains no mention of any form of punishment (Whitwell, 1927). Neither does Marie Louise Rames' diary, written between the ages of 13 and 14 in 1843 (Rames, 1911). Anna Catherina Bower, born in 1768, went to school in Salisbury until age of 12 and then completed her education in London. She commented how happy she was at school (Bower, 1903). Similarly, Caroline Head born in 1852, was sent to boarding school at 13 and liked it (Head, 1905). The value system of the eighteenth and especially the nineteenth century, with its stress on obedience and duty, certainly encouraged the reliance on corporal punishment more than today. Teachers who wished to wield the rod could do so, not with impunity, but with the tolerance of society. Whippings and humiliation were not, though, common to all schools and all teachers.

In the past, there was less listening to children and more regulating of them. Education was conceived of as a passive process: the instructor imparted and the children absorbed the lessons. Pupils were meant to conform to the system rather than the other way around. Although attempts were made to grasp the personality of each child, this was more to do with finding the best method to convey education rather than tailoring a programme to fit an individual child's needs. In the eighteenth and nineteenth centuries, children could be bored and, worse, could be brutalised. However, they could also appreciate the opportunity to learn, and if they had the good fortune to be taught by a good teacher, children could revel in the learning experience. It was the teacher's personality rather than the child's which would dominate the relationship.

CHAPTER 3

Children's Education: A Test Case for Best Interests and Autonomy

Michael Freeman

With the formulation of the United Nations Convention on the Rights of the Child and with the passing of the Children Act 1989[1] the debate about children's rights has taken on new significance. Although in England the signs were already there with the Gillick decision in 1985,[2] particularly with Lord Scarman's emphasis on an adolescent's decision-making competence being tied to understanding and maturity rather than chronological age, autonomy has come to the fore in the Convention and the Children Act. Yet the old equation of children's rights with protecting their welfare, with their best interests, also remains in both of these normative statements. Has the debate then been resolved in an unsatisfactory compromise or can the two views stand together? And what are we to make of Education Acts and accompanying literature which seem to ignore the newer focus altogether, or a least underplay it? This chapter addresses these issues. But first, why is it important to think that children have rights?

Why rights are important

Rights are important – few would deny this. They have been called `valuable commodities',[3] they are important moral coinage. They 'enable us to stand with dignity, if necessary to demand what is our due without

---

Unlike other chapters, references here follow the Oxford system, and references and notes are to be found at the end of this chapter.

having to grovel, plead or beg'.[4] Rights are entitlements: they are not dependent on the discretion or choice of the official or bureaucrat in control, of the teacher, the education department or the court. And rights we cherish have largely been fought for (the vote, trade union power, the right to be free from corporal punishment at school). They are rarely 'given' without a struggle. If we have rights, we are entitled to respect and dignity and no amount of benevolence, charity or compassion is an adequate substitute for this.

Towards children's rights

The struggle for rights long ante-dates any recognition that children might also be rights-holders. Early legal statements are conspicuously silent on children's rights: the 'Ten Commandments', arguably the most influential of all legal codes, contain a clear normative pronouncement on parent-child relations ('Honour thy father and mother...'), but it is framed in terms of respect for parents and is silent on the obligations of parents to love and nurture children. Is it surprising then that, as Richard Helmholz[5] has found, well into early modern times children were being prosecuted in England before ecclesiastical courts for abusing parents, but prosecutions of parents for beating children appear not to have taken place?

One of the earliest recognitions of children's rights is found in the Massachussetts *Body of Liberties* of 1641: parents are told not to choose their children's spouses and not to use unnatural severity against their children. Children, furthermore, are given 'free liberty to complain to the Authorities for redress'. But this is also the law (and is better known for so being) that prescribes the death penalty for children over 16 who disobey parents. Note, even 350 years ago, protection of children went hand-in-hand with adding the power of the state to parental authority.

The next two centuries can hardly be said to be identified with children's rights. There are concerns to protect children, though these are often clumsy or inchoate. It is pertinent to observe that the documents emanating from the great libertarian revolutions, the American and the French, have nothing specifically to say about children. The nineteenth century saw the birth of the child-saving movement, the growth of the orphanage, the development of schooling and the construction of separate institutions, including the juvenile court, for delinquent and neglected children.[6] Child protection legislation was introduced more than 60 years after legislation to protect domestic animals, and even then not without resistance.

It was at this time, at the end of the nineteenth century, that lone voices began to advocate children's rights as amounting to more than protection or salvation: writers such as Kate Douglas Wiggin in the United States, better known for her children's stories; Janusz Korczak in Poland, also a children's writer, and later to gain eternal fame in the Warsaw Ghetto. Wiggin's view of childhood, a century ago, is refreshingly modern. I like her espousal of 'the divine right to be gloriously dirty' justified as a 'necessary consequence of direct, useful, friendly contact with all sorts of interesting, helpful things'. Wiggin was an early advocate of the abolition of corporal punishment. 'It seems likely', she wrote in 1892, 'that the rod of reason will have to replace the rod of birch'.[7] Korczak[8] formulated his ideas during the First World War. *How to Love a Child* took as one of its main theses the idea that you cannot possibly love a child – your own or another's – until you see him or her as a separate being with the inalienable right to grow into the person s/he was meant to be. Korczak claimed that 'respect for the child' was the basic requirement of an educator: where this was particularly novel was that he formulated this as a 'right'.[9] More than half a century was to elapse before others began to recognise the importance of a child's 'autonomy', or even the significance of 'respect'.

Early declarations

The first international declaration (the Declaration of Geneva of 1924) was more limited in its aspirations. Its preamble states that 'mankind owes to the child the best it has to give'. Its five terse principles emphasise welfare: the requisite means for normal development, food and medicine, relief in times of distress, protection against exploitation, and socialisation to serve others. There was no specific reference to educational rights. It was another 35 years before children's rights received international recognition again. We get considerable insight into attitudes towards children's rights in the late 1950s – when civil rights issues were only beginning to make an impact – from the discussions which took place at this time. The French delegate to the Commission on Human Rights in 1959 believed that 'the child was not in a position to exercise his own rights' and that a 'child had special legal status resulting from his inability to exercise his rights'. Despite ideological conflicts, divisions between what we would now call 'North' and 'South', and religious divides, only Cambodia and South Africa were unable to agree the UN Declaration of the Rights of the Child of November 1959. The ten principles adopted included for the first time in an international instrument the right to education. The principles adopted were:

1. Non-discrimination.
2. Special protection and opportunities to develop physically and mentally, morally, spiritually and socially in a healthy and normal manner and in conditions of freedom and dignity.
3. A right to a name and nationality.
4. The right to the benefits of social security; adequate nutrition, housing, recreation and medical services.
5. The right of a special needs child to the treatment, education and care required by his particular condition.
6. The need for love and understanding so that the child, wherever possible, is to grow in the care and responsibility of his parents, and in an atmosphere of affection and moral and material security.
7. Entitlement to education, free and compulsory, at least in the elementary stages.
8. To be among the first to receive protection and relief.
9. Protection against all forms of neglect, cruelty and exploitation, including that associated with employment.
10. Protection from practices which may foster racial, religious and other forms of discrimination.

It will be observed that, though its scope is more extensive, the emphasis is still firmly on protection and welfare, on 'the investment motive'. There is no recognition of a child's autonomy, no understanding of the importance of a child's wishes, and no appreciation of the concept of empowerment. The child remained an object of concern rather than a person in his or her own right. It is therefore not surprising that education is identified with schooling rather than recognised in any broader sense.

The liberation movement

In the decade immediate following, the world woke up to the evils of discrimination, initially against blacks and other ethnic minority groups, and then against women. Within a decade, this consciousness of discrimination had embraced the status occupied by children. The term 'liberation' emerges for the first time as a sub-title of an article in a collection entitled *Children's Rights*, published in 1971.[10] Writing in this book, Robert Ollendorf argues for the adolescent's rights to self-determination and to participation. This reads today as an extraordinary essay, a diatribe against 'Authority' and 'the Establishment' by a psychiatrist who grew up in Hitler's Germany. He sees rightless adolescents taking their revenge on society as women 'who were rightless and sexless chattels' are now 'outbitching the sons-of-the-bitches'. He calls for the adolescent to have 'a right to find his own way and determine on his own how he is going to learn, what he wants, what he rejects, what kind of art he likes, what kind of art he dislikes, what books he wants to read, in which way, if any he wants to worship'. He demands society embrace a willingness to allow adolescents to participate in decision-making concerning themselves. The manifesto looks rather tame now but at the time the book, oozing the sentiments of Summerhill and Woodstock, was thought radical, if not outright dangerous.

The writings of John Holt[11] and Richard Farson[12] had a greater impact, though in Holt's case it was his books on schooling which attracted greatest attention.[13] It was self-determination that Farson saw as at the root of all other rights that children were entitled to claim. Responding to the anticipated criticism that such rights might not be 'good' for children, he argued:

> asking what is good for children is beside the point. We will grant children rights for the same reason we grant rights to adults, not because we are sure that children will then become better people, but for more ideological reasons, because we believe that expanding freedom as a way of life is worthwhile in itself. And freedom, we have found, is a difficult burden for adults as well as children.[14]

Farson, in *Birthrights*, lists nine rights, all of which he sees as derived from the right to self-determination. They are:

1. The right to alternative home environments allowing the child to 'exercise choice in his own living arrangements'.
2. The right to information that is accessible to adults, for example the right to inspect records kept about them.
3. The right to educate oneself: he favoured the abolition of compulsory education. This right includes freedom from indoctrination, with children choosing their own 'belief systems'.
4. The right to sexual freedom: pornography would be made available to children as it is to adults, and children would be allowed to

experiment with their sexuality without fearing punishment.

5. The right to economic power, including the right to work, to develop a credit record and to achieve financial independence.
6. The right to political power, including the right to vote. Nothing, he suggests, indicates that children will 'vote less responsibly than adults'.
7. The right to responsive design.
8. The right to freedom from physical punishment.
9. The right to justice.

Holt's list is not dissimilar, but it includes also the right to travel, to drive (why should this be tied to age rather than ability to pass the driving test?), and to use drugs.

It is easy to ridicule some of what Farson, Holt and the rest of the liberation school of the 1970s wrote, and, indeed, it has been criticised.[15] But it must be remembered that when they wrote, child sexual abuse had yet to be 'discovered', and drugs were not seen as the social problem they constitute today. Attitudes to pornography were also very different. We would want to protect children from premature exposure to sex and from contact with drugs. Indeed, we might look askance at the attitudes to work and education that we find in these charters. But protection was not in the vocabulary of the 1970s' advocates. Thus, Holt, writing of drugs, says: 'I don't think that we should "protect" children against whatever drugs their elders use, and in a society in which most of their elders do use drugs and many use them excessively and unwisely, I don't see how we can'.[16]

The argument for liberation

It is worthwhile going back to the child liberationist literature to explore the arguments posited in it for child liberation. In part it attacks what it sees as the false assumption that there are morally relevant differences between children and adults. The central morally relevant difference is, most would say, the capacity for instrumental rationality. But proponents of child liberation are not convinced that this constitutes a satisfactory dividing line. Thus, John Harris points out, quite rightly, that there are 'bold, quick, ingenious, forward and capable young people' and neither they nor 'dull-witted, incompetent adults' are a 'rarity'.[17] The principle of universalisability is thus said to mandate equal rights.

Howard Cohen's *Equal Rights for Children*[18] appears to be similarly based but ultimately turns on a utilitarian judgement that the possible harm of giving children equal rights would not outweigh the benefits provided by those rights. This latter justification is countered by Onora O'Neill[19] who claims that the costs of seeing children's rights as fundamental outweigh the advantages. O'Neill prefers to look to the obligations of others towards children: a construction made from the agent's perspective may, she believes, deliver more. But O'Neill cannot be right to assert that the child's 'main remedy is to grow up'. This underestimates the capacities and maturities of many children. Both in moral and cognitive development, many children reach adult levels between 12 and 14, though the ability to reason may increase through adolescence.[20] We are prepared to impose criminal responsibility on 10-year-olds,[21] even, it seems, to lock them up. Petitions to the Home Secretary indicated a groundswell of opinion favouring life imprisonment for the 10-year-old murderers of James Bulger. But we are less willing to accept the correlativity of responsibility and rights. O'Neill also ignores the impact on adult life that parenting and socialisation leave: persons, deprived of rights when children, will grow into different adults from those upon whom rights have been conferred.

But whether self-determination is or is not a good idea, it remains the fact that those who drew up the UN Convention and those who wrote our latest Children Act were convinced, or partly convinced, of the importance of the recognition of autonomy.

The UN Convention on the rights of the child

Thirty years separate the UN Declaration and the UN Convention on the Rights of the Child. The thinking of the period in between is to some extent reflected in the differences. Philip Veerman is surely right to characterise the Convention as 'an important and easily understood advocacy tool – one that promotes children's welfare as an issue of justice rather than one of charity'.[22] The Convention contains:

1. General rights, such as the right to life, prohibition against torture, freedom of expression, thought and religion, the right to information and to privacy.
2. Rights requiring protective measures, including measures to protect children from economic and sexual exploitation, to prevent drug abuse and other forms of neglect and abuse.

3. Rights concerning the civil status of children, including the right to acquire nationality, the right to preserve one's identity, the right to remain with parents, unless their best interests dictate otherwise, and to be reunited with their family.
4. Rights concerned with development and welfare, including the child's right to a reasonable standard of living, the right to health and basic services, the right to social security, the right to education (though an attempt to extend this to pre-school education was resisted on economic grounds) and the right to leisure.
5. Rights concerning children in special circumstances or 'in especially difficult circumstances', such as handicapped children, refugee children and orphaned children. Included are special regulations on adoption, the cultural concerns of minority and indigenous children, and rehabilitative care for children suffering from deprivation, as well as a prohibition on the recruitment of soldiers under the age of 15.

The Convention goes beyond earliest formulations, which stressed the duties of adults and of the state (or 'mankind'), to emphasise child participation in decision-making. It is the first convention to state that children have a right to 'have a say' in processes affecting their lives. The child, notes Marta Pais,[23] is thus conceived of as a 'principal' in the Convention.

Article 12, the article providing for a child's participation in decisions affecting him or her is, I believe, the linchpin of the whole Convention. It will surely prove the most significant. It is a development from the child liberation philosophy of the 1970s. It is in line with the Gillick decision in the House of Lords in 1985 and, as already indicated, is one strand in the latest Children Act. The Article states:

1. States Parties shall assure to the child who is capable for forming his or her own views the right to express those views freely in all matters affecting the child, the views of the child being given due weight in accordance with the age and maturity of the child.
2. For this purpose, the child shall in particular be provided the opportunity to be heard in any judicial and administrative proceedings affecting the child, either directly or through a representative or an appropriate body, in a manner consistent with the procedural rules of national law.

The right enunciated here is significant not only for what it says, but because it recognises the child as a full human being, with integrity and personality and the ability to participate fully in society. It is important, as John Eekelaar[24] acknowledges, that 'the generality of the first paragraph of this article should not be overshadowed by the particularity of the second'. The first applies to 'all matters affecting children', where children's views should be given 'due weight'. The views of children are to count when decisions ranging from education to the environment, from social security to secure accommodation, from transport to television, are being taken. It is much easier to pick up on the second paragraph and expostulate on Gillick and the Children Act than to recognise the real shortcomings in our approach to the ideals of the first paragraph.

Article 12 is a key provision and it gets ideological support from the two articles which follow it: article 13 which constitutes as part of 'freedom of expression' 'the right to seek, receive and impart information and ideas of all kinds', and article 14 which emphasises 'freedom of thought, conscience and religion'. But attention has also focused on Article 3 which states, in its first paragraph, that:

> In all actions concerning children, whether undertaken by public or private social welfare institutions, courts of law, administrative authorities or legislative bodies, the best interests of the child shall be a primary consideration.

Articles 12 and 3 encapsulate a tension in the whole debate which has been examined here. Article 12 emphasises the centrality of a child's views: Article 3 the priority to be given to concerns of welfare. The principle in Article 3 is not overriding (a Polish attempt to make welfare paramount failed), but its imperative and the philosophy of Article 12 are in potential conflict. Eekelaar sees in the second paragraph of Article 12 a 'counterweight' to the welfarist concerns of Article 3. But the conflict is a real one, as has been seen in England in recent years as the implications of Gillick are teased out in the interplay with real-life problems of anorexic[25] and psychotic adolescents.[26]

Which children's rights?

So there has been talk of children having rights for about a century. Early discussion focused on child salvation, on furthering the individual child's welfare. Only in the 1970s did the movement to liberate children emerge; only then did we begin to view children as persons rather than social problems.

Rights perform various functions.[27] The protective rights can be divided into rights against the world and rights of protection from inadequate care. 'Liberating' rights may be subdivided into conferring adult legal status and rights against parents.

Children's rights against the world assert the general importance of providing them with the conditions they need to flourish, although no specific persons are entrusted with this duty ('Mankind owes...' – as the Geneva Declaration put it). Rights against inadequate care, however, do assign duties to particular individuals. But these kinds of rights assume that children's incapacities warrant special protection. They protect by providing for goods and services normal adults must procure for themselves. They also protect by frustrating children's desires when these conflict with what those 'protecting' children consider to be their immediate or long-term good. In this sense we protect children by making them go to school, because we believe that education is for children's benefit both now and in the long-term. Children may not want to go to school but we say their desires will stultify their future development. We may be wrong – indeed, some believe we are – but most of us tend to say this nevertheless.

'Liberating' rights, by contrast, facilitate the opportunities for children to act upon their desires. Such rights presuppose that their subjects know what they are doing when they choose to exercise them, even if doing so is risky to themselves or harmful to others. Many adult rights are of this kind: adults can legally vote, drink, have sexual relations, choose medical treatment and commit themselves to binding contracts concerning work, marriage and make other financial arrangements. The absence of such rights in children either precludes or renders illegal such acts for them.

Too much of the literature on children's rights has dichotomised. There have been the child salvationists and the child liberators.[28] A division has been created between those who, to quote Farson, wish to protect children and those who wish to protect children's rights.[29] There is a 'nurturance' orientation and one which emphasises 'self-determination' or autonomy.[30] There is general acceptance of the importance of protection rights, though there remains dispute as regards their content. But on the question of autonomy there is less agreement.

To believe in autonomy is to believe that anyone's autonomy is as morally significant as anyone else's. And autonomy does not depend on the stage of life that a person has reached. The extent to which we allow them to exercise it may, but that is a separate question. There is considerable convergence of legal and philosophical thought about what it is about human beings that makes them persons. For Haworth it is 'critical competence',[31] for Lindley it is a capacity for reasoning.[32] These tests are not unlike that constructed by Lord Scarman in the Gillick case. Lord Scarman offered no guidelines as to when a child reached what we now call 'Gillick-competence', and, in terms of age, legal commentators since have assumed that this was reached during adolescence. It is, however, clear, once criteria for personhood are examined, that many children acquire critical competence considerably earlier. I think a good account of the criteria is articulated in Lindley's *Autonomy*. He says:

> Certainly consciousness is a requirement. More specifically a person is a creature which has beliefs and desires, and acts on its desires in the light of its beliefs. However, this is insufficient for personhood. What is required in addition is the capacity to evaluate and structure one's beliefs and desires, and to act on the basis of these evaluations'.[33]

He also approved Frankfurt's account of freedom of will and the concept of a ``person'.[34] According to Frankfurt, to be a person, a creature must have 'second-order volitions', that is desires about which desires she wants to become her will. For Lindley, 'people have will, insofar as they do not necessarily act on their strongest inclinations, but have the general ability to act on the results of their deliberation'. He argues that a crucial requirement is the possession of the concept of 'a self': someone has to be able to think of himself 'as a being with a future and a past, a subject of experience, a possessor of beliefs and desires'. It is not clear exactly when children acquire these concepts, and there may well be gender and class differences, but at 7 it would not be uncommon, and at 10 it may be thought that most children have become persons in the sense depicted here.

Limits on a child's autonomy

To respect a child's autonomy is to treat that child as a person, and as a rights-holder. It is clear that we can do so to a much greater extent than we have assumed hitherto. But it is also clear that the exercise of autonomy by a child can have a deleterious impact on that child's life-chances. It is, of course, true that adults make mistakes (and also mistakes when interfering with a child's autonomy), but having rights means being allowed to take risks and make choices. As Ronald Dworkin has famously announced, if we take rights seriously we must accept that rights-holders will sometimes do things that we do not think are good for them (or perhaps even for us).[35]

There is reluctance to interfere with an adult's project. This reluctance is tempered when the project pursuer is a child by the sense that choice *now* may harm choice *later*. To Loren Lomasky, 'what counts as damage...is determined by what will likely further or diminish its eventual success in living as a project pursuer'.[36] This is to recognise that children are different. Many of them have lesser capacities and abilities. Many of them are more vulnerable than adults. They need protection. If welfare rights are not recognised, they will not be in a position to exercise autonomy. All this is true, but it is not as true as we have come to believe. Children are different, but they are not all that different. There is a 'developmental trajectory' through which we all pass. Age is often a suspect classification. If we are to apply a double standard, we must justify it. Double standards are not necessarily unjustifiable: things which appear to be different may, on further reflection, not be as different as they looked initially. The onus lies on those who wish to discriminate. Hitherto, they have not discharged this burden very convincingly. How many of the structures, institutions and practices established, it is said, to 'protect' children, have actually done so. Think of the youth (juvenile) court. The care system. Observation and assessment centres. Reporting systems where abuse has been identified. Child protection registers for children 'at risk'. Indeed, many practices within the education system. The official version of the truth rarely withstands critical examination. But ask also whether, and to what extent, we are prepared to encourage children to participate in decisions regarding their life choices. It is much easier to assume abilities and capacities are absent, than take cognizance of children's choices.

It is the argument of this chapter that the moral integrity of children needs to be recognised, that we must treat children as persons entitled to both equal concern and respect, with entitlement to having both their present autonomy recognised insofar as it exists, and their capacity for future autonomy safeguarded. And this is to recognise that children, particularly younger children, need nurture, care and protection.

In looking for a children's rights programme, we must thus recognise the integrity of the child and his or her decision-making capacities, but also note the dangers of complete liberation. Too often writers on children's rights see rights in 'either-or' terms: there is either salvation or liberation, nurturance or self-determination. But to take children's rights more seriously requires us to take more seriously both the protection of children and recognition of their autonomy, both actual and potential.

Inevitably, this imposes limitations on a child's autonomy. The paternalism that we associate with protectionists offers a framework for seeing autonomy as well. We cannot allow children the autonomy to indulge in actions or activities which will irreparably damage their full lives as adults. There is a case for intervention in children's lives to cushion them against irrational actions. But what is to be regarded as 'irrational' must be strictly confined. The subjective values of the would-be protector cannot be allowed to intrude. What is 'irrational' must be defined in terms of a neutral theory capable of accommodating 'pluralistic visions of the good'. Nor should we see an action as irrational unless it is manifestly so in that it would undermine future life choices or impair interests in an irreparable way. Mistakes must be tolerated: we cannot treat persons as entitled to equal respect without respecting their capacity to take risks and make mistakes. We would not be taking rights seriously if we only respected autonomy when we considered the agent was doing the right thing. But we would also be failing to recognise a child's integrity if we allowed an action – using heroin or perhaps choosing not to attend school – which would seriously and systematically impair the attainment of full personality and development subsequently. I say 'perhaps' because there may well be circumstances where not attending school is the right decision for a particular child. Education is a 'good' that we would want for every child: schooling may not be.

The test of 'irrationality' must also be confined so that it justifies intervention only to the extent necessary to obviate the immediate harm, or to develop the capacities of rational choice by which the individual may have a reasonable chance of avoiding such harms.

Liberal paternalism

The question we should ask ourselves is: what sort of action or conduct would we wish, as children, to be shielded against, to mature to a rationally autonomous adulthood and be capable of deciding on our own system of ends as free and rational beings? We would, I think, choose principles that would enable children to mature to independent adulthood. One definition of irrationality would be such as to preclude action and conduct which would frustrate such a good. Within the constraints of such a definition we would defend a version of paternalism, namely, 'liberal paternalism'.[37] This version of paternalism is a two-edged sword in that, since the goal is rational independence, those who exercise constraints must do so in such a way as to enable children to develop their full capacities.

All paternalistic restrictions require moral justification. In many cases it is not difficult to adduce sufficient and convincing reasoned argument. It is not difficult to present the case for protecting children against actions which may lead to their death or to serious physical injury or mental disability. Nineteenth-century legislation which made it illegal for children to go down coal mines or up chimneys or into factories can thus be defended – though such legislation may not have been passed to protect children. So can laws designed to protect children from sexual abuse and exploitation. There are clear dangers in the suggestions of writers of the 1970s like Farson and Holt that a child's right to self-determination includes a right to a sexual relationship with whomsoever he or she pleases. The 'discovery' of sexual abuse in the 1980s has all but put an end to these demands. On the other hand, 'ages of consent' as such are meaningless: the crucial factor is the presence or absence of exploitation, so that the age *difference* may be of greater significance than the age of the child. A system of compulsory education and restrictions on employment can also be defended, though the content and goals of 'education' would need examining through the prism of children's rights, something all too rarely attempted.[38]

What should legitimise all these interferences with autonomy is what has been called by Gerald Dworkin, 'future-oriented' consent.[39] The question at its simplest is: can the restrictions be justified in terms that the child would eventually come to appreciate? Looking back, would the child appreciate and accept the reason for the restriction imposed upon him or her, given what he or she now knows as a rationally autonomous and mature adult? This is not an easy test to apply. It involves something close to what Derek Parfit has called, 'ideal deliberation'. As he puts it:

> What each of us has most reason to do is what would best achieve, not what he *actually* wants, but what he *would* want, at the time of acting, if he had undergone a process of 'ideal deliberation' – if he knew the relevant facts, was thinking clearly, and was free from distorting influences.[40]

This raises many questions. What are the 'relevant' facts? How are hypothetical preferences to be considered? Can distortion of values be eliminated? The answers are not simple; we would not expect them to be. But they are questions worth pursuing for out of the answers will come greater insight in how to understand childhood, its freedoms and its constraints.

And education?

It is a matter of some puzzlement how, in the general thrust to actualise children's rights, there should have been such an obvious neglect of them in the sphere of education. In these days of citizens' charters, when we are all 'consumers', those who have conceived our almost annual Education Acts have put parents rather than children in the forefront. The Acts are Acts which enhance parents' rights, not children's. Whatever the issue in question it is not the opinion of children which is sought.

How is one to explain this? A trite, and incomplete, answer may be sought in the different personnel, experiences and ideologies of the different government departments involved. The role of the different professionals involved – social workers and teachers – may also be part of the explanation: social workers intervene in families at the point of dysfunction where questions of rights are more to the fore; the teacher's interaction with children is on a day-to-day basis where 'superficially' no issues of law arise. This is, of course, not true, but then the lawyers' image of law as pathological rather than constitutive ('a programme for living together')[41] has perhaps left its mark on the public too – it is all too easy to think that the law plays no part in life until something goes wrong. It may also be that rights issues are to the fore more obviously in the child care field where adults are often fighting over possession of a child, seeking a residence order or a care order, than in the sphere of education where, ironically, it may be thought that 'only' a child's soul is being contested. A further possible explanation is that, rightly or wrongly, child care issues have seemed more controversial (for example, do social workers have too much power or too little?). Education, by contrast, has been treated almost as unproblematic. It is surely significant that the right to education, though unquestioned, has become identified with the right to schooling,[42] though clearly it is very different, broader and less contentious.

And yet the rights issues in education are so pervasive, as one would expect within the confines of a 'total institution' often committed to conformity and always to socialisation.[43] But what say have we given children over the content of education? Issues such as sex education and religious education remain matters of political debate – the essentially Christian school assembly is a contested space as I write[44] – but children, whose wishes and feelings are considered elsewhere, remain on the sidelines here. Both in the development of the National Curriculum and the introduction of testing of children at particular ages, the children themselves have been objects of intervention, never participants in social processes which affect them. The rights of ethnic minority children, trampled upon by governments unwilling to fund their schools, have been given no opportunity of expression of opinion as to the propriety of schooling that we might not think good for them but they might find culturally valuable. The wearing of school uniform, of badges, ear-rings, turbans and *kippot*, compulsory school sports, cadet corps and many similar questions raise children's rights issues and invariably in debates about them, where such debates even take place, children's voices are silenced.

The most recent education act and the documents accompanying it – the Education Act 1993, its Code of Practice and the Regulations and Guidance for Parents on the Special Educational Needs Tribunal (established in section 177 of the 1993 Act) – are similarly neglectful of a rights perspective which is open to participation by children. The Code of Practice states five fundamental principles: these address welfare and needs questions, articulate those considerations that the Department for Education considers to be in the best interests of children with special needs, and cite last that 'the knowledge, views and experience of parents are vital'.[45] Note there is no reference to the knowledge, views or experience of children. To read this sentence is to be reminded of standard attitudes of the past. It is as if ministers and civil servants in the Department for Education were completely oblivious to the guidelines in the Children Act. Is it thought in the DfE or by the government that Gillick-competence does not extend to matters of education? If the wishes and feelings of children are relevant in matters which come within the scope of the Children Act (see s. 1 (3) of that Act), why should this not be the case with education decisions too? There is evidence, confirmed by the Elton report, *Discipline in Schools* and OFSTED reports on disaffected pupils and on behaviour in schools, that pupils behave more responsibly if they are given more responsibility and treated with respect. Further, since education is clearly 'a matter affecting the child', it is difficult to see how the government can think the Act is not in breach of Article 12 of the Convention. But the government apparently thought the idea of inserting a provision in the 1993 Act referring to 'ascertainable wishes and feelings' of the child was 'dotty' and to be condemned as 'politically correct'. It even thought the provision unnecessary in the light of the Children Act. In coming to this conclusion they ignored the advice of a leading QC that the 'Children Act does not provide for Article 12 to have effect in respect of any of the relevant education matters'.

The Code goes on to acknowledge that 'effective assessment and provision will be secured where there is the greatest possible degree of partnership between parents and their children and schools, LEAs and other agencies'.[46] This is expressed clumsily: is the partnership to be between parents and their children or parents and children and schools? The latter is the more likely interpretation but either way it is easy to imagine a conflation of the wishes and views of children with those of their parents. Why was no thought given to the independent representation of children when this concept is so key to the processes of the Children Act 1989?[47] It is true that the Code goes on, in listing the practices and procedures essential in pursuit of the principles, to admit that special educational provision is most effective when those responsible take into account `the ascertainable wishes of the child concerned, considered in the light of his or her age and understanding'.[48] The ontological status of the child's wishes should be noted: they are to be taken account of because they may produce better decisions, not because it is normatively right to do so. If it were thought to be so, we can assume it would have featured in the principles too. And why, it may be asked, does the Code refer only to `wishes' and not to 'wishes and feelings'? The latter expression has become a term of art[49] and is anyway particularly apposite where persons with special needs are concerned – they may be more readily able to express feelings than articulate wishes. Oddly, this is acknowledged later in the Code where schools are told to `make every effort to identify the ascertainable views and wishes'[50] of the child or young person about education matters. And further, in listing the benefits of involving the child, the Code supplements the utilitarian consideration (effectiveness) with the normative consideration of principle. 'Children', it says, 'have a right to be heard. They should be encouraged to participate in decision-making about provision to meet their special educational needs'.[51] It recognises the part participation can play in improving self-image and boosting confidence.[52] If you treat persons as human beings they may behave accordingly: reify them and you can expect them to behave as 'problems'. If these matters are important, why are they not recognised as principles? Why are they not 'up-front' in the Code? The symbolic importance of so doing cannot be underestimated. That its significance was not appreciated is an indictment of our policy-makers. Their guilt remains even if later paragraphs mitigate it somewhat. The Special Educational Needs Tribunal is similarly flawed for, although we are told the Tribunal 'may wish to take account of the ascertainable views of the child and, on occasions, hear evidence from the child', there is no obligation to do so and it will 'normally only seek evidence from the child with the parents' consent'.[53] No provision is made for the child to be independently represented.[54] The new *Guidance* on 'How to Appeal' to the Special Educations' Needs Tribunal does, however, state that `if your child want[s] his or her views to be taken into account separately from your own views, your child can attend the hearing and answer questions as a witness; or make a written statement.[55] Hesitant moves are thus being made to recognise the importance of the child as a participant in decision-making.

An interim report on the Department for Education and its role as a propagator of children's rights could offer no more encouragement than 'Beginning to see the issues as long last: could do much better'. But there is a ray of hope for the future – a future which, it may be predicted, will be better for children and better for the rest of us when we finally acknowledge that children are persons whose rights must be endorsed.

Notes

1. On which see M.D.A. Freeman, *Children, Their Families and the Law* (London: Macmillan, 1992).
2. [1986] A.C. 112.
3. By Richard Walserstrom, (1964) 61 *Journal of Philosophy*, 628, 629.
4. Per B. Bandman (1973) *Proceedings of the 29th Annual Meeting of Philosophy of Education Society*, 234, 236.
5. (1993) 1 *International Journal of Children's Rights*, 23.
6. On which see A. Platt, *The Child Savers* (Chicago: University of Chicago Press, 1977).
7. Children's Rights: *A Book of Nursery Logic* (Boston, Houghton, 1892).
8. On Korczak see the fine biography by Betty Jay Lifton, *The King of Children* (London: Hodder and Stoughton, 1987).
9. And see P. Veerman, *The Rights of The Child and The Changing Image of Childhood* (Dordrecht, Martinus Nijhoff, 1992, ch. VII).
10. Edited by P. Adams *et al* (London: Granada, 1972).
11. *Escape from Childhood* (Harmondsworth: Penguin, 1975).
12. *Birthrights* (Harmondsworth: Penguin, 1978).
13. *How Children Fail* (New York: Dell, 1964); *How Children Learn* (Harmondsworth: Penguin, (revised) 1991).
14. *Op cit*, note 12, p. 31.
15. For example by Laura Purdy, *In Their Best Interests?* (Ithaca, Cornell University Press, 1992).
16. *Op cit*, note 11.
17. In K. Graham (ed.) *Contemporary Political Philosophy: Radical Studies* (Cambridge: Cambridge University Press, 1982).
18. (Totowa, N.J.: Littlefield, Adams, 1980).
19. (1988) 98 Ethics 445.

20. See the excellent critique by Tom Campbell in P. Alston *et al* (eds), *Children, Rights and The Law* (Oxford: Clarendon Press, 1992).
21. The Divisional Court recently, even disposing of the *doli incapax* presumption which has existed since the fourteenth century or before. See C v DPP [1994] 37 All E.R. 190. 'But the House of Lords has now restored the presumption, whilst recommending its removal by legislation. See [1995] 2A II ER 43'
22. *Op cit*, note 9.
23. *Bulletin of Human Rights*, 91/2 (1992), pp. 75, 76.
24. In *Op cit*, note 20.
25. *Re W* [1992] 4 All E.R. 627.
26. *Re R* [1991] 4 All E.R. 177
27. See M.D.A. Freeman, *The Rights and Wrongs of Children* (London: Frances Pinter, 1983), ch. 2.
28. See C.R. Margolin (1978) 22 *Social Problems* 441.
29. *Op cit*, note 12, p. 9.
30. See C.M. Rogers and L.S. Wrightman (1978) *Journal of Social Issues*, 34, 59, 61.
31. *Autonomy: Essay in Philosophical Psychology and Ethics* (New Haven, Yale University Press, 1986).
32. *Autonomy* (Basingstone: Macmillan, 1986).
33. *Ibid*, p. 122.
34. (1971) 68 *Journal of Philosophy*, 5.
35. *Taking Rights Seriously* (London: Duckworth, 1977).
36. *Persons, Rights, and the Moral Community* (New York, Oxford University Press, 1990).
37. *Op cit*, note 27, pp. 54 – 60.
38. But see G. Haydon (1993), *International Journal of Children's Rights*, 1, 213.
39. In R. Wasserstrom (ed.), *Morality and The Law* (Belmont, Calif: Wadsworth, 1971, pp. 107, 108).
40. *Reasons and Persons* (Oxford, Oxford University Press, 1984).
41. *Per* Lon Fuller (1969) *American Journal of Jurisprudence*, 14, 1.
42. See I. Illich, *Deschooling Society* (Harmondsworth: Penguin, 1973). See also R. and W. Stainton Rogers, *Stories of Childhood* (Hemel Hempstead: Harvester Weatsheaf, 1992).
43. For a historical perspective see H. Hendrick in A. James and A. Prout (eds) *Constructing and Reconstructing Childhood* (London: Falmer Press), 1990, pp. 35, 45–7.
44. *The Independent*, 1 June 1994.
45. Department for Education and Welsh Office, Code of Practice on the Identification and Assessment of Special Educational Needs (London: DFE, 1994, para. 1.2).
46. *Idem.*
47. See Children Act 1989 s. 41.
48. *Op cit*, note 45, para. 1.3.
49. See Children Act 1989 s. 1(3).
50. *Op cit*, note 45, para. 2. 36.
51. *Ibid*, para. 2.35.
52. *Ibid*, para 2.36.
53. Department for Education, *Special Educational Needs Tribunal – Consultation Paper on Draft Regulations and Rules in Procedure* (London: DFE, February 1994, para. 40).

54. See the proposed Regulation 7. On children's rights in this area, see further M. John (1993) *International Journal of Children's Rights*, 1,1.
55. Special Educational Needs Tribunal: *How To Appeal*, 1994, p. 11.

Part III
The voice of the child in school

CHAPTER 4

Listening to pupils in classrooms and schools

Tony Charlton

Policies and practices in education are renowned for their inconstancy. Often they change like shifting sands, responding to public opinion, current academic wisdom and political and social whim. Many changes are sensible and shrewd, implemented with care and sensitivity; others generate only disquiet and frustration. Occasions arise, however, when innovation is applauded almost universally.

This chapter discusses one such innovation where teachers are becoming more aware of, as well as responsive to, their obligations to heed opinions and other disclosures from their pupils.

Background

The notion that children have rights is a relatively recent one, its emergence linked to a broader concern with human rights. Whilst both strive to advance and protect the rights of individuals, some of these rights still remain unrecognised or largely ignored. In the case of children, for example, people often worry about the degree to which adults respect youngsters' rights to have their feelings, opinions and views heeded by them. This concern has been heightened by cases involving the police, social services and other child-care personnel, where these rights appear to have been disregarded or dishonoured. It is unsurprising, therefore, that children's rights have now become a focus for attention in education just as they have in social services, health, the judiciary and policing. Ron Davie reflects the mood of the moment when he talks about this thinking as 'currently pushing at the frontiers of good practice in education...' (1993, p.52).

There are many reasons for heeding pupils' communications. We listen to them because we want to know more about them so we become better able to understand and to help them. On other occasions we listen because they need to talk about a concern or fear. In these instances we listen because someone has to, so youngsters can 'release' the problem, talk about it and hopefully resolve it. There are times also when we listen so we can diagnose, and help remove, learning blocks which prevent pupils from successfully acquiring academic skills. There are occasions also when we listen because we value their involvement in school affairs. By listening to their views we extend our knowledge of *their* perceptions of those experiences. If we listen carefully we may learn more about our own successes and failures; and we should be prepared to consider changes in our provisions and practices in the light of such comment. More recently, the notion of self-assessment has attracted interest.

Whilst we may not always feel there is time to listen to them in these ways, it is right that we should, just as it is their right to be heard. Children's rights are unlikely to be upheld if adults ignore or reject these responsibilities. Teachers, therefore, hold important responsibilities for helping to ensure that children's rights are upheld.

This chapter considers a number of educational practices which provide opportunities – and responsibilities – for teachers and others to heed pupils' views upon matters related directly, or otherwise, to their schooling. It is not always easy to find the time, or the energy, to listen actively to groups or individuals, although this difficulty becomes more understandable (though not more acceptable) when we appreciate the complexity of the listening skill.

The skill of listening

Listening – like conversation – does not happen easily in today's frenzied world. Exacting demands linked to many of our work, family and social settings can leave little time for interpersonal exchanges. Perhaps, also, listening is taken for granted; underestimated, undervalued and oversimplified. Yet listening is a highly complicated skill. According to Mehrabian (1972), a communication is conveyed only partly by words; in fact he contends that only 7 per cent of a message is conveyed in this way. The remaining 93 per cent comprises voice tone (38 per cent) and body language (55 per cent). In a similar vein Bolger (1975, p. 168) talks about listening,

> not just with our ears but with our eyes, so that we perceive facial expressions, gestures, eye-movements, posture... . Tiny changes in the

> eyelids are valuable clues – a slight widening when he is frightened and a slight closing when hostile or thoughtful.

Clearly, listening is an intricate and elaborate skill which underpins and facilitates many interpersonal communications. Notwithstanding the complexity of the listening skill, and the time-constraints imposed upon them in their work, teachers still find time to listen to their pupils.

Listening to pupils

Listening to children is a fundamental component of good teaching, irrespective of the age of the pupils. Consequently, it is unremarkable that it permeates so much of the teacher's work, both inside and outside classrooms. However, as noted earlier, making time to listen to pupils can be difficult in busy classrooms. Furthermore, the considerable amount of time *teachers* spend talking in classrooms can sometimes obscure the important role listening plays – or should play – in helping to educate children and young adults. Whilst a lot of talk takes place in classrooms, teachers appear to monopolise nearly 70 per cent of this discourse. Even when children *are* allowed to speak, their contributions tend to be 'in a context highly constrained by the teacher, such as in answers to closed questions' (Kyriacou, 1986, p.144). Although teacher talk unquestionably can be a major component of good teaching, there is a danger that we fail sometimes to appreciate the benefits of teachers developing and practising listening skills. For a variety of reasons (which we shall turn to later) we want to encourage our children to talk, yet they remain unable to do so if we monopolise available time with *our* talk. We need to enable *pupils* to speak and this can be achieved with the help of our 'listening skills and sensitivity' (Owen, 1991, p.308).

When time and facilities are available for pupils to talk, teachers can learn much from tuning in to their pupils. This learning is not confined only to aspects of the pupils' academic performance, personality or behaviour. Given appropriate encouragement, pupils can also provide opinions on a range of matters to do with the school's and teachers' performance. McKelvey and Kyriacou (1985), for example, note that pupils' assessment of teachers' lessons provides 'teachers with valuable information and insights into their own teaching' (p.23).

Practising basic counselling strategies with pupils encountering personal difficulties, supporting their academic strivings, expressing an interest in their welfare and seeking their views about matters to do with school's administration and organisation, provide but cursory examples of activities within which teachers may need to apply their listening skills. We now consider, in more detail, ways in which schools and teachers may listen to pupils' feelings and opinions.

Listening and counselling

For many pupils the teacher is someone whom they can turn to with their concerns, fears, worries and anxieties. It is remarkable that teachers are so often successful in these situations, for their pre-service training rarely equips them with even the most rudimentary counselling skills (David and Charlton, in press). We are not talking here about complex counselling skills but about relatively simple, yet effective, approaches which can be used by teachers to help their pupils. There are many approaches which lend themselves to school or classroom encounters of this type, but one which fits well with teachers is Carl Rogers' (1951) client-centred model. Part of this appeal stems from its avoidance of counsellor advice *directing* clients towards problem resolutions. Just as inviting, perhaps, is that (on the client's part) it is a talking therapy whilst the counsellor's contribution is primarily a listening one. The counsellor strives to create a climate which enables the client to feel free to talk about her or his problems. Through efficient use of active listening skills, teachers demonstrate they want to listen, are trying hard to share (or empathise with) the pupil's thoughts and feelings, and want to help. A lot of this interest and support is conveyed via non-verbal communications. On other occasions the teacher makes use (sparingly) of verbal comments to maintain, explore and encourage (or seek clarification about) the pupil's talk.

Approaches of this kind are about the teacher engaging in active listening with a pupil who thinks or feels (s)he has a problem. The teacher uses tactics, such as those below, to encourage pupils to talk about, and hopefully resolve, their problem:

Some verbal communications

Clarification

Pupil:	So she used to ignore me deliberately.
Teacher:	She deliberately took no notice of you?

Encouragers

Pupil:	(Silence)
Teacher:	Tell me more about how you felt.

Gentle nudgers

Pupil	I felt that she..she..
Teacher	You felt that she...?

Maintainers

Teacher	Right/ uhh huh/ umm/ I see/ good.

Some non-verbal communications

Raised eyebrows:	sharing surprise
Frown:	sharing concern
Smile:	sharing pleasure or humour
Shaking head:	sharing disapproval
Nodding head:	sharing approval or agreement
Eye contact:	I'm here, with you.

Of course talking by itself is often therapeutic; it helps the individual to 'get it out of her system'. But we should not underestimate the listening aspect of this helping process, because it is often the key to success. Some teachers take a long time to acquire, or feel easy with, these active listening skills. Often this difficulty arises because teachers expect to do most of the talking; it's not always easy for them to remain silent and listen to pupils. Thus, another benefit which teachers gain from learning more about non-directive counselling skills is that they may become more inclined to introduce active listening into their teaching repertoire. (Listening to pupils' contributions may be more instructive, and enlightening, at times than listening to teachers!)

McIlvain (1992) focuses upon problems associated with teacher talk. She is critical of her own classroom work where she practises teacher talk which is 'dominating and managerial' (p.52). She suggests this type of talk discourages child-initiated talk and leaves little time or opportunity for listening on the teacher's part. She utilises strategies drawn from non-directive counselling in order to encourage child talk. By adopting what she refers to as 'puzzled listening', she encourages her children to talk not only to her but also to their peers.

In recent years non-directive counselling skills have also proved successful, in helping pupils whose difficulties in learning seem to derive from an emotional block in their learning pathways. It is well worth looking at some of these occasions to examine how the listening skill plays a major role in helping these children to become more successful in their academic work.

Listening and supporting pupils

There are many instances in classrooms where the 'teacher's ear' provides help to children's learning: listening by the teacher supports learning by the pupil. Of course this link is probably true in many areas of the teacher's work, but here we are concerned with occasions where pupils' anxieties, low self-image and fears handicap their learning. In these instances instructional work is unlikely to succeed until therapeutic intervention removes the handicap (or emotional block, as it is sometimes called). More often than not, this intervention incorporates skills more readily associated with non-directive counselling strategies than teaching practices. Whilst these strategies require teachers to empathise with the pupil, it is the listening facility which anchors them (Burns, 1982). During the last 20 years or so the value of this 'listening and talking' therapy has become clearly established. Teachers use their listening skills to encourage children to talk about themselves in ways which help remove blocks to learning. More innovative, perhaps, are those instances when peer counsellors have been involved in this work. Experiences have shown that peer counsellors are often as successful as their adult counterparts in undertaking non-directive support work with pupils (James *et al*., 1992).

One of the pioneers of this type of intervention with learning difficulties was Lawrence (1971; 1972) who maintained that his pupils' reading failure was often a consequence of unresolved emotional concerns caused by repeated academic failure. The primary school children had developed negative beliefs (e.g., a low self-image) about their ability to learn successfully. To remove the emotional concerns, Lawrence planned his intervention to reopen the learning pathways. He did this by utilising non-directive counselling techniques with 'counsellors' who often had little or no prior knowledge of counselling strategies. The counsellors were equipped to:

- become sympathetic, non-judgmental listeners
- attend with interest to pupils' talk
- encourage students to talk and express views and opinions
- show those views and opinions were valued.

Whilst the listening skills are clearly explicated in the first of these requirements, they are also implicit in the other three. How can you show someone you are interested in what (s)he is saying unless you express this directly – or indirectly – through your listening stance? It is crucial in this sort of work that you show the pupil 'you are interested in what she has to say and that you are taking it seriously' (McIlvain, 1992, p. 52). Along similar lines, Melissa (1992) argues that we should not only listen to pupils' fears and believe them; more importantly we should also 'display this belief' (p.18). As Lawrence demonstrates in his research, good listening skills are invaluable ways of demonstrating that another's talk is valued. Similarly, McMurray (1986) talks about practices in his classroom where:

> A good deal of importance is attached to listening and responding sympathetically to pupils' talk .... Pupils are helped to be made aware of their worth by knowing that people feel they are worth listening to (p. 35).

Where this awareness is developed, teachers can gently nudge children to reflect further upon their concerns so pupils can, themselves, help remove emotional blocks to learning. Burns (1982) talks about this process as giving a type of cathartic release. Finally, the outcomes of Lawrence's research should be noted. He found many of his pupils' reading skills improved when they were given opportunities for someone to listen to their feelings. This facility enabled them to gain support and understanding, improve their self-image and rekindle their lost feelings of confidence and competence.

These listening-oriented strategies have been incorporated into other programmes similar to Lawrence's, where pupils' poor learning seemed to be due, at least in part, to emotional blocks (Murfitt and Thomas, 1983; James *et al.*, 1992). A few of these studies incorporated a novel approach by using pupils' peers to administer the intervention. Some justification for this type of involvement is given by Quarmby (1993). Using young secondary school pupils to successfully counsel peers with bereavement experiences, he noted that although: 'the skill of active listening is one that is normally considered difficult to acquire ... it seemed to come naturally to these young people' (p. 203).

James *et al.* (1992) showed this peer involvement facility has distinct benefits in secondary schools where it is often difficult for teachers to find time to undertake one-to-one counselling. Twelve senior pupils were recruited to act as peer-counsellors to 12 younger peers experiencing difficulties with their learning. Counsellors were selected because their teachers felt they had natural attributes which would assist them to help others. Attributes included being good listeners and having the ability to make good relationships. Counsellors were then trained in the very simple counselling techniques which Lawrence had used. The training stressed that not only should they listen attentively, but also that they should show that they were listening by employing appropriate facial and body expressions (e.g., mirroring surprise, excitement, concern, interest). Once again the counselling intervention was successful in improving the counsellees' reading and spelling performances.

As mentioned earlier in this chapter, it is only in recent times that there has been a conscious attempt on the part of schools to listen meaningfully to pupils with the intention of using their contributions to help shape school policies and practices. It is worth looking at one or two of those initiatives.

Heeding pupils' contributions

Recently, a trend has emerged where many schools take more heed of pupils' opinions and experiences by providing them with meaningful involvement in school affairs. Pupils are more likely to develop a healthy interest in school matters if they have some say in what happens to them, and their self-esteem can be enhanced. Schools can also learn to appreciate that their pupils' experiences in school are a valuable knowledge source.

There are various ways in which this 'tapping' can take place. Usually this happens where conscious efforts are made to provide meaningful opportunities to listen to, and respond to pupils' views, opinions and suggestions on school matters, including procedures, policies and curricula (e.g., Garner, 1992; Blatchford and Sharp, 1994). Whilst involvement of this type does not suggest a full partnership between teachers and pupils, it does suggest pupils' feelings and opinions are being valued and utilised. Involvement along these lines helps expunge ill-conceived assumptions that pupils are able only to function as pawns in the educational process. Movement towards this type of partnership is unlikely to be well-received by those supportive of more traditional and dated practices where pupils remain subjugated to the whims and wishes of teachers. Mindful of this problem, Cowie (1994) talks of teachers who distrust students to behave responsibly, and consequently prohibit moves towards greater involvement by them. Other barriers to pupil involvement are noted by Sharp and Blatchford (1994) who caution that with 'the imbalance of power in schools, the participation of pupils carries the greatest risk of superficial involvement' (p.191).

Concerns such as these are best answered with instances where pupils' contributions have been heeded and proved useful. Cowie (1994), for example, makes reference to two initiatives where pupils effected successful changes within their school. Both initiatives utilised the

Quality Circle (QC) concept drawn from industry. The concept requires a small group of people (in this case, pupils) to meet on a regular basis to identify problems within the school such as bullying or inadequate playground facilities. Solutions to problems are suggested and discussed within the QC group before being presented to management (i.e., teachers and the headteacher).

In the first study, primary school children suggested improvements were needed to reduce problems in the playground such as bullying and boredom. The children consulted among and outside their QC group to discover ways in which playground facilities could be enhanced. Then they outlined plans for changes, wrote to local businesses for help and presented progress reports not only to their group but also to the school assembly. Outcomes from the QC group included a recommendation to the headteacher that the physical design of the playground should be changed (e.g., new layouts, new markings). Additionally, pupils produced booklets on playground games with step-by-step instructions. Not content with this they also arranged for demonstrations of the games to take place during the break periods.

In the other study (Sharp *et al.*, 1994), secondary school pupils were involved in the successful development of a whole-school policy on bullying; they also participated in the formation and implementation of (what they termed) a 'bully line'. The objective behind this initiative was:

> to offer a listening service for pupils in the school. The pupils negotiated clear ground rules to achieve their aim of providing a safe forum where pupils could talk freely and explore possible solutions. If necessary, they were eager to act as advocates for the bullied pupil by telling a member of staff what was happening to them, or perhaps by accompanying the bullied pupil whilst they themselves told a member of staff. (Cowie, 1994, p.164).

Both studies suggest benefits. Schools benefited from heeding pupils' experiences and suggestions and by empowering them to become actively involved in initiatives. Pupils gained from their involvement in a number of ways. They acquired new skills with help from their teachers and enhanced self-esteem through their participation and successful outcomes. In the case of the bully line initiative it was particularly pleasing to note the comments of Sharp *et al.* (1994, p.5) that the ways in which the peer counsellors 'proved to be utterly responsible and reliable' had:

> paved the way for the pupils to take more of a managerial role for the bully line over time. The pupils have decided to set up a management committee

where pupils organise fund raising, advertising, role planning and administration.

Elsewhere, studies have listened to pupils' comments on a range of other school issues including discipline (Garner, 1992), rewards and punishment (Harrop and Holmes, 1993), and changing school (Wade and Moore, 1994). Interestingly, the first two studies were consistent with the spirit of the recommendations by the Elton Committee (DES, 1989b) that pupils should become more active in 'shaping and reviewing the school's behaviour policy' (p.144).

More extensive consultations were incorporated in the Keys and Fernandes (1993) study. This latter enquiry asked over 2,000 pupils in Years 7 and 9 to comment on their experiences in, and attitudes towards, school. For the most part pupils' responses were illuminating; on occasions they were also disturbing. For example, only marginally more than half of the pupils reported that all, or most, of their teachers praised them when they worked well. Of more concern was the finding that nearly half of the pupils said they never, or hardly ever, talked to teachers on their own about their work. Other findings showed that a quarter of the older pupils (half of the Year 7 pupils) had truanted at some time and a third of Year 9 pupils admitted being bullied in the last year. That some of these findings were greeted with surprise by teachers can only add credibility to the view that listening to pupils enhances our knowledge and understanding of their perceptions of school.

One value of obtaining children's perceptions of their school experiences is that they provide at least a cursory indication of their account of their treatment and behaviour in school. Given recent emphases on accountability and appraisal exercises in schools, it would be imprudent if these exercises failed to provide facilities to listen to client opinion. However, a word of caution is worth noting here. Where teachers' perceptions of pupils' experiences in school conflict with pupils' perceptions we should refrain from hastily accepting the former rather than the latter. Discrepancies may arise, as Harrop and Holmes (1993) found in their enquiry, because teachers sometimes have difficulty in perceiving accurately pupils' thoughts and feelings. In Harrop and Holmes' study, Year 5 and 6 pupils from two schools were asked to rank classroom rewards and punishments according to the degree to which each motivated them to work and behave. At the same time teachers were required to rank the items according to how *they* thought the children would respond. Unexpected outcomes showed that whilst:

> pupils were tending to rank the rewards and punishments in the same ways, irrespective of gender or school, ... teachers were not tending to rank the rewards and punishments in the same ways as their pupils. (p.32).

Mindful that teachers' work is influenced strongly by their perceptions of its efficacy, Harrop and Holmes conclude that their findings are worrying given that, 'views and practices must inevitably be linked' (p.35). Their findings can only add support to calls for teachers to listen more to their children.

Writing within the context of what he sees as a consumer-led society Garner (1992) also stresses the wisdom of consulting pupils in order to gain information about their school experiences. In his investigation he asked pupils to list their preferred learning experiences and teaching styles. This action is particularly useful with pupils who are considered to be disruptive. Listening to and, where practicable and desirable, acting upon these preferences should increase teachers' (and pupils') opportunities to make the learning process 'a more meaningful and rewarding activity' (p. 404). Sometimes we can be motivated to ignore, or discount, the other's point of view. At other times this neglect occurs because we undervalue potential outcomes from listening to others' comment about our performance in the workplace or elsewhere. Yet this other viewpoint is important. It can encourage us for the best of reasons to question what we are doing, as well as how and why. The young children of Barbiana had such oversight in mind when they wrote to their teachers:

> People who get no criticism do not age well. They lose touch with life and the progression of events. They turn into poor creatures like yourselves. (Barbiana, 1969, p.29).

Different reasons for heeding pupils can be found in the BATPACK training materials (Wheldall and Merrett, 1982). Primary school children's help is enlisted in formulating four positive rules for behaviour in classrooms. There are at least two reasons why this conferring has success potential. First, pupils are involved in a decision-making process which has direct implications for the regulation of their behaviour; there is a sense of autonomy here which will not go unnoticed by many pupils. Second, if the pupils are meaningfully involved in the exercise then it is likely that subsequent rules are going to be understood and supported by them.

Adults can become forgetful about (and insensitive to) ways in which particular school-related ordeals arouse fears among children. The primary/secondary transfer is one event which is a stressful experience for many youngsters (and their parents). In their enquiry, Wade and Moore (1994) demonstrated how well children can remind us of these types of experience, if we listen to them. They consulted over 150 children with a wide range of special needs about their views of changing schools. Responses showed that over half of the sample expressed fears about being lonely, not being able to make new friends, being bullied or picked on, not coping with academic work or about harsh teachers. Children with visual impairments expressed fears about finding their way in unfamiliar buildings. From a more positive perspective the children suggested ways in which the transfer could be less anxiety-provoking. Their comments demonstrate a sensitivity and sensibility which may shame some schools. Pupils suggested that before pupils move to a new school the teachers at the new school should:

- tell you what it is like
- have things ready
- show you around
- be aware that you're coming
- let you have a day there
- let you meet the teachers
- know what a difficult and painful experience it is.

This last comment is particularly sensitive and mature. It helps illustrate the value of heeding children's views. If we wish to plan better for children's needs, there is much to commend initiatives like this one. The researchers conclude their report by stating that:

> By taking note of these views, those concerned could help facilitate the change for children with special needs...It is our view that the majority of their (the children's) responses indicates that they have a right to participate in any decision making concerning choice of school for them (Wade and Moore, 1994, p. 27).

It is to be hoped that initiatives of this kind will become more commonplace in the future. The notion of pupil participation should become enhanced if school inspections incorporate a meaningful response to OFSTED requirements that inspection evidence shall include some 'discussion with pupils' (1995, p. 14).

Listening to self-assessments

It has been a customary practice in schools – though an uncommon one –

to heed pupils' self-assessments on such matters as their emotional functioning (e.g., their feelings about their self and their anxieties). However, the practice of listening to pupils' self-assessments in academic (and academic-related) areas is more recent and more embryonic.

Within the past few decades initiatives such as the Certificate of Pre-Vocational Education (CPVE), the Technical Vocational Education Initiative (TVEI) and Record of Personal Achievement (RPA) have included a trend towards pupil profiling, of one type or another. In accord with the DES (1989c) policy statement on records of achievement, these innovations offer opportunities for older pupils to become involved in 'self-assessment and in the discussion of their assessment with their teachers' (Murphy and Torrance, 1988, p.36). It is worth noting that Rogers (1983) suggests this involvement necessitates an unlearning process – rather than being a *learning* one – where pupils are encouraged to become less dependent upon external sources for evaluations (e.g., from teachers or through peer comparisons) and more inclined to look 'inward for signs of progress and growth' (p. 62).

However, opportunities for meaningful self-assessment are not as common as they should be. Whilst this paucity may stem from schools' failure to empower pupils to undertake self-assessments, it may reflect a disbelief on the part of teachers that pupils can undertake such evaluations even though experience has demonstrated that pupils (both young and old) *can* engage successfully in self-assessment practices and that these practices have the potential to produce great gains for pupils and teachers alike (Barsby, 1991; Blatchford, 1992; Boud, 1992; Towler and Broadfoot, 1992). This is particularly the case in secondary schools where Records of Achievement became an important vehicle for assessment and where there is evidence that self-evaluation has beneficial outcomes upon such matters as pupils' awareness, motivation and involvement in their work (DES, 1988). It appears these outcomes have been noted within a number of National Curriculum documents where it is suggested that pupils should describe and record their own progress.

The interest which secondary schools have invested in self-assessment has been matched less frequently in primary schools, even though the process of helping young children to assume responsibilities for assessment and record-keeping facilitates a practical and manageable way of helping teachers to cope with the demands of National Curriculum assessment. However, there is evidence of trends towards self-assessment practices which are achieving both popularity and success with younger pupils. Blatchford (1992), for example, found that older primary school pupils were more than capable of assessing their own academic ability especially when 'accuracy of self-assessment was assessed in terms of agreement with standardised tests' (p. 41). Elsewhere, Barsby (1991), whilst cautioning that pupils need help and support in order *to acquire* self-assessment skills, talks of the many gains from such practices with 7-year-olds, including increased motivation to work and greater independence of the teacher. In a similar vein Towler and Broadfoot (1992, p.138) note that:

> Reflection and evaluation can encourage understanding of what is expected, improve motivation, lead to a positive influence upon teaching style and management in creating a more truly democratic partnership between teacher and children.

Despite the positive nature of the above discussion, the notion of listening in the classroom to pupils' own evaluations of their learning experiences and associated progress is one which has not always been translated meaningfully and successfully into primary and secondary school practices. Schools, teachers and pupils still need further guidance if the value of such practices is to be realised. Some staff may need to be convinced of the potential value of this type of listening; many may require help so they can equip their pupils with the skills needed to become involved. Furthermore, along the lines suggested by Rogers (1983), pupils are likely to require assistance to 'unlearn' prior practices where they were overly dependent upon external sources for information about their learning achievements. It may be the case that these matters can best be addressed successfully where discussions and outcomes concerned with self-evaluation are 'grounded in a whole school approach' (Towler and Broadfoot, 1992, 150–51).

To conclude

Active listening (in an interpersonal context) is rarely given the recognition and time it deserves in classrooms and schools, or elsewhere. This is regrettable for a number of reasons, as this chapter has sought to make clear. Children stand to derive much benefit from being listened to: their academic success can be improved, their personal problems can be reduced, their self-esteem and motivation can be enhanced. Schools benefit too.

It is perhaps initiatives to involve children in decision-making processes which encounter most resistance. Staffroom diehards may point out that children lack the skills and experience to become involved in this way. This may be the case. It may also be that this unpreparedness exists because schools have been unable, or unwilling, to provide opportunities for pupils to acquire the skills and experience needed. What is unquestionable, as the work reviewed in preceding pages has shown, is that children respond favourably and successfully to challenges of this type. It is to be hoped that other schools will take note of their colleagues' successful undertakings in these areas, and by recognising the considerable benefits that emanate from them, begin to make their own arrangements to listen more attentively to their pupils. A reluctance to heed children in these ways is irresponsible and is neglectful of what is one of their basic rights.

CHAPTER 5

Personal Development, Pastoral Care and Listening

Michael Marland

Introduction

There are five axioms for the place of listening to children in primary and secondary schools:

- Listening to children is not an occasional special activity as a reaction to crisis, but a necessary thread of the whole school's educational delivery.
- Just listening is insufficient: it will not be fully effective unless pupils are helped to reflect on, analyse and express their feelings and concerns.
- Like other aspects of personal and social education and pastoral care, it has a curriculum aspect: pupils need teaching to develop concepts, attitudes and skills if they are to benefit from the activity.
- Institutional planning of staff roles, relationships and opportunities is necessary for success: sensitivity requires systems.
- Finally, it contributes to the central aims of schools and the legislative requirements of them.

The possibilities are more optimistic than cynics would suggest. Teachers are not despised by pupils as hopelessly distant. Indeed, pupils regard teachers as possible listeners. It is perhaps surprising how well most pupils regard their teachers from this point of view: 70 per cent of pupils in a very large sample of secondary students reported that they 'get on well with most or all of their teachers'. Offered the choice of whether 'the school and they are like good friends, friends, distant relatives, strangers or enemies', it might be surprising to some that over half of the pupils placed their school in the first two categories, with another quarter 'distant relatives', and only 10 per cent 'strangers' and 6 per cent 'enemies' (Barber, 1994, p.1).

Statutory obligations

Although only the statutory orders for Special Educational Needs and Exclusions specifically require the views of pupils to be heard, it could also be argued that a school has a statutory curriculum obligation to embody communication in the educational delivery. The overarching requirement for the curriculum is to prepare the pupils for 'the opportunities, responsibilities and experiences of adult life' as the Education Reform Act 1988 stresses it (Section 1, para.2(b)). Communication is clearly a key component of all three, and expressing one's own view of one's self is an important aspect of that. Listening and reacting are both important, but communication breakdown also derives from the inability of so many to shape and articulate their feelings, a proper approach to listening.

The more specific National Curriculum requirements also include this ability, with the English orders including the requirement that the school should 'develop pupil's abilities to communicate effectively in speech and writing and to listen with understanding'. This is not merely a part of the English course leading to GCSE, but an essential and major part of that broader requirement of preparation for 'opportunities, responsibilities and experiences'.

This demand for communication is now reinforced by the terms of OFSTED inspections. These do not evaluate the educational delivery of the NC merely subject by subject; in addition, the observation and evaluation criteria that inspectors are obliged to follow (laid out in the *Framework* part of the *Handbook*, include the following crucial definitions of part of 'pupils' spiritual, moral, social and cultural development':

> Social development is to be judged by how well the school prepares pupils for relating to others in different social settings, taking responsibility, exercising initiative, working successfully in groups and participating co-operatively and productively in the school community, and how well the pupils respond (HMI, 1994, p.21).

These ambitions cannot be achieved without education in communication.

Although the central reason for these demands on the school curriculum is the long-term social skills of the pupil for adult life, they require the teaching and practising of skills for the pupils' present needs: the pupil who cannot talk cannot be listened to, and therefore can be less well helped.

Adult apprenticeship

Our approach to bringing up children in families, schools, and society more generally, has since the 1960s over-emphasised the peer group. In a laudable endeavour to normalise socially the perceived rarefied and impersonal school, 'master-centred' schools were replaced by 'peer-group oriented' ones.

We have emphasised, indeed since Plowden (CACE, 1967) startlingly over-emphasised, the value of the peer group. In so doing we have so often locked the child into 'the prison of the peer group' (Alec Dickson's powerful phrase) and denied child-adult interaction, and thus adult listening. The young need more time with adults: 'In middle childhood, survival and life skills, along with morals and manners, go on being learned over at least five more years of close apprenticeship to adults' (Leach, 1994, p.xv). 'Apprenticeship' requires listening, and gives valuable adult models.

Meeting the child's needs

The two extremes of how to establish the best support for a child are both inappropriate: basing it only on what a child says he or she needs or working only from preconceived adult definitions. On the one hand there is a true sense in which the 'adult knows best' – the adult has seen more and can foresee a great deal. On the other hand, the young person's experience and perception can refine, deepen and illuminate the adult wisdom.

Thus, finding ways of listening is a way of strengthening school planning. 'Part of becoming an adult as a result of progressing through school life', says John Bazalgette (1982), is taking up a pupil role which 'is constantly open to revision as judgements about oneself and one's context change over time'. Listening by the school is a key part of this, and is essential to finding ways of meeting the widest possible range of a child's needs. That process of 'becoming an adult' requires self-analysis:

> The process depends upon a growing capacity for awareness of oneself, one's capacities, feelings, beliefs and values and a growing ability to make judgements about one's context, its possibilities, threats, differences and similarities (Bazalgette, 1982, p.12).

The crucial definition of Article 12 of the UN Convention on the Rights of the Child (c.f. Freeman, Chapter 3) is that the state:

> shall assure to the child who is capable of forming his or her own views the right to express those views freely in all matters affecting the child, the views of the child being given due weight in accordance with the age and maturity of the child.

This requirement needs to be built into a school's aims, structures, staff roles, and pupil curriculum and pastoral care. As Penelope Leach so cogently puts it:

> It is social policy that in all its dealings with children, society should give priority to 'the best interests of the child'. But who is to judge the 'best interests' of the particular individual if nobody listens to her? (Leach, 1990, p.179).

The planning of every aspect of the school should take into account the views of the pupils. This does not mean adapting completely, but recognising the most potent ideas.

Crises

There are times when listening has an especial urgency for most of the school community. There will be occasional catastrophes and deeply distressing events. The possibility of a school being shattered by a major crises is rare but real. The Aberfan coal-tip tragedy in 1966 killed 166 children and 28 adults. Since then there have been many different school-focused tragedies. Have we learnt how to enable the individuals, the families and the school community to cope? The aptly titled Gulbenkian study *Wise Before the Event* (Yule and Gold, 1993) analyses the needs and gives succinct advice. Teacher-listening is a key element of the school's necessary response, and needs advance planning:

> After a disaster pupils as well as staff may feel enormous pressure to talk about their experiences. After a few days this can become irritating for those young people who were not involved. Initially adults should listen, no matter how disruptive it is to the task in hand; after a few days the young people should be encouraged to talk to a designated member of staff, although the

> young people themselves should obviously have some say in the choice of listener (Yule and Gold, 1993, p.35).

Skills need to be articulated and shared in readiness; for instance, knowing when to prompt and when to enable. Yule and Gold admirably express the tension between reticence and encouragement:

> A perceptive teacher is not intrusive, and knows when to talk and when to listen. When a child looks distressed or, uncharacteristically, has gone quiet over several days, then the perceptive teacher may take that child aside and ask what he or she is feeling. Experience has shown that children will not talk about their innermost feelings to parents and teachers unless they are given strong signals that it is safe to do so. Plenty of time must be allowed once the child starts to unburden. A word of warning, however – teachers need to obtain 'permission' from the child to talk this way (op. cit., p.36).

Special sessions will have to be arranged and outside counsellors sought. 'Debriefing' is a bureaucratic term, but useful as a concept for the structuring of listening. Yule and Gold again:

> Debriefing is a way of talking about not only what happened but of sharing the often frightening emotional reactions to the events. By holding a debriefing meeting in the school, usually led by an experienced person from outside, the school is giving the pupils and staff permission to exchange their reactions and educating them in how best to cope in the period that follows. A separate debriefing meeting may be necessary for staff who are directly affected by the crisis (op. cit., p.38).

Education choices and the child

Whereas for most children schooling appears as a series of insistent demands lacking the choices of their peer-group life, there is in fact a number of key choices. Children can choose books to read from their first year in the infant school, and the educational value of topic work in the junior years is greatly enhanced when children play an active part not only in its planning but also in its assessment. In the secondary years, there are choices of subject and decisions about projects for GCSE. These 'choice steps' require subtle adult listening. They are both important for effective next steps, and also as part of growth. Not only does such listening usually enhance the efficacy of the choice, but it also educates the child: to be listened to, participate, and have views taken into account and acted upon is to become more understanding of society, decision-making and self. The choices the pupil has to make in education are a paradigm of life's choices.

Perhaps choice of infant or junior school cannot much involve child views, but it can somewhat. Certainly it should in primary-secondary transfer, when a real choice is technically possible. Consider the process of choosing a secondary school. The statutory wording uses only the term 'parent', yet in very many cases the choice is jointly made between child and parent. Michelle de Leo's recent research found that a very large proportion of choices in the London area were perceived by the pupils as having been made by parents and children jointly (de Leo, 1994). Both primary and secondary schools should recognise this in their procedures, however modestly. For instance, when families visit North Westminster as part of their secondary-school selection, I try to ensure that I ask the girl's or boy's interests, whether they have any questions, and their views.

The same is true of the GCSE option process in the secondary school at the end of Key Stage Three. The offering of, preparing for, and exercise of 'subject choice' has two complementary but equally important purposes: to facilitate the best range of courses and to engage the pupil in an experience of adult life – making choices. Neither of these aims will be achieved if the young person is not listened to. Yes, we often to a considerable extent do 'know what's good for you', but this needs to be tested against 'what you say you need'. These are complementary. Thus schools should:

- Develop choice opportunities as extensively as practical.
- Prepare for these choosing processes as fully as possible.
- Plan for staff-student counselling and listening opportunities.
- Have clear and closely promulgated staff roles and structures.
- Build in reflection opportunities after the choice.

Obviously the same is true of post-16 choices and A-Level courses. Even at pre-university preparation and choice it needs emphasising. The UCAS procedure incorporates a personal statement by the student-applicant. However, do we always give pre-university the fullest opportunities? At North Westminster we have a 'Personal tutor' system, so that each student has an experienced teacher working in his or her own way with that student, and the choice is mutually made: the tutee chooses the tutor, who can decline. Mutual talk is the core of the work.

Special Educational Needs and the statutory processes laid down in the Code of Practice (DfE, 1994a) may seem quite different, but the Code requires children's points of view to be considered formally. A school's

SEN policy should ensure that this is done sympathetically and efficiently. It is rare for a Statutory Instrument to so precisely require us to listen to children:

> The effectiveness of any assessment and intervention will be influenced by the involvement and interest of the child or young person concerned. ... Schools should, therefore, make every effort to identify the ascertainable views and wishes of the child or young person about his or her current and future education. Positive pupil involvement is unlikely to happen spontaneously. Careful attention, guidance and encouragement will be required to help pupils respond relevantly and fully ... (DfE, 1994a, pp.14–15).

For many it is more unexpected that these children ('of all our pupils!') should be listened to. Schools must 'have regard to' the principle that the child has a right to be heard. This may not quite be a statutory right, but it is getting close.

Finally, exclusion is another choice option in which the pupil's perspective must be taken into account. The procedures for the governors' 'consideration' are derived from the Education Act 1993 and interpreted in a DfE (1994b) Circular. it requires the governing body to convene a meeting with at least three governors present and to 'give parents the opportunity to make written and oral representation in an environment which avoids intimidation and excessive formality' (p.16). Whilst pupils are not specifically included in that reference, the circular does imply the presence of pupils and their rights by stating: 'The governing body should also advise parents and pupils that they may if they wish have someone of their choice to accompany them and assist them at the meeting'. (DFE, 1994 b). Even in the painful process of considering exclusions, the pupil should be clearly given a voice.

Main requirements for a 'listening school'

A successful 'listening school' needs several aspects of its work to be appropriate. The solution is multi-factorial, and no single scheme can create it; these include the following.

Attitudes

If a high proportion of staff consider most of the time that pupils are present they should only be taught a narrow course curriculum, the pupils will have little opportunity to talk and be listened to. Staff attitudes are the basis of the school's work, and the core of this is the formally articulated school aims. A properly agreed and promulgated description of the aims can be used to inform and encourage staff attitudes, as well as developing procedures and creating opportunities.

Structures and staff roles

Goodwill and skills are necessary but are not sufficient: even the most skilful and well-meaning teacher or support staff member cannot often be effective if the opportunities have to be struggled for and if there are not clear communication lines. The following section analyses this in more detail.

Staff skills

The skills of listening, enabling the pupil by a well-judged question or prompt, and responding by look and word do not merely 'come naturally'. Not only do they have to be worked at, but in-service work can usefully be part of a school's professional development programme.

The curriculum

There is a rarely articulated and still less argued assumption that listening to children is just done if you intended it, requires only the adults to have the right attitudes and skills, and is an aspect of pastoral care quite independent of the curriculum. The contrary is true: pastoral care has to have a substantial curriculum content if it is to be proactive and not merely reactive (c.f. Marland, 1989b; 1995). Pupils require a range of learnt attitudes, concepts and skills if they are to be sufficiently self-understanding, analytic and expressive to communicate sufficiently fully. There is always of course something to listen to, react to and make positive use of. However, as in health and law, for instance, the more insightful and articulate the 'client', the more likely the professional is to be able to hear. The curriculum implications include self, opportunities and communication – about all of which much can be and needs to be taught and learnt.

Those four complementary aspects of the school's policies, structures and procedures all need consideration from the specific point of view of encouraging significant listening to pupils.

Roles and responsibilities: the staff team

The trouble with the key notion of everyone contributing is that it can lead to no one taking significant responsibility. This is a particular problem for the generalist class teacher in the primary school. The generalist can only work effectively if specialist guidance and support are available. The school must plan its staff roles and responsibilities.

Every teacher must be a listener, but particular roles, and the relationship between them, need defining. The essential point is to identify the key teacher so that the pupil knows to whom to turn and the teacher knows she or he has this responsibility. In the primary school it will virtually always be the class teacher and in the secondary school the tutor. The first is largely accepted but the great expansion of pastoral care understanding in the last decade has not helped all schools clarify and support the role of tutor, and initial training is often weak on this aspect.

'A tutor is a teacher whose subject is the pupil herself' (Marland, 1989b, p.iii), and the same applies to the class teacher in a primary school. I will develop this argument with respect to the secondary school tutor, but the same principles apply to the work of the primary class teacher. The centre of the tutorial role is enabling the pupil to understand him or herself more fully, assess attainment, and plan ways forward. Self-understanding, social skills, communication skills and all aspects of interpersonal skills are the heart of tutoring.

Although individual meetings are valuable and, indeed, essential, the bulk of the work has to be carried out in the full tutor group. The axiom I have therefore developed is that 'the art of tutoring is helping the individual without relying entirely on individual help'. This involves using full-group discussion to complement individual case-work by giving opportunities to explore personal and social topics through a 'tutorial programme' of discussion material (c.f. Marland, 1989a). If a pupil is to control his behaviour, he needs to be self-aware, and part of this is to be able to stand outside himself, as it were, and look afresh at himself almost as a spectator. The temptation is always to go straight into group discussion: 'What do you think about . . .?' on a range of personal and social matters. However, such a topic requires also a brief presentation of actuality through text, visual image, or sound. For instance, a discussion of 'To what extent do boys and girls differ in their feelings?' needs to mix personal reminiscence and observation with statistics. The pupils are listening to each other but the use of facts will have prompted a fresh set of ideas. The tutor needs to find a scheme for the planning of meetings, which need to be full-group, small-group and individual. These should not be merely reactive but also planned as 'review sessions', that is, regular private meetings in pleasant surroundings which are conducive to relaxed talking and listening. The need is to create a relatively safe environment. Such occasions allow the child to talk as a pupil unstressed by a specific event or an impending decision. Even if these are in a tutor group of, say, 30 only once a term, such a routine review session has a strength for listening which is denied to the emergency meeting to cope with a problem. The pupil talks better and the tutor listens better on the occasions when she is stressed by difficult or unhappy events if she has had such 'review' meetings. For the first one-to-one talking and listening to be at a crisis is to make it much harder for the pupil to talk.

Fairly often the tutor or pastoral team leader will invite a pupil's parents to the school for a meeting, and sometimes the young person speaks differently in this group than with the teacher on his own. Indeed, the child-parent group sometimes leads the pupils to revelations, ideas, or comments that might not arise otherwise.

Indeed, for this listening reason home visits have some special advantages. Of course, the presence of parents can create an inhibition. Nevertheless, because the teacher is the 'guest' and the family in control of seating, refreshments and atmosphere, children will often be not so much more forthcoming as *differently* forthcoming. I judge that I have fairly often heard things said by pupils when I have been talking in their homes that I should not hear in school – and that we have all benefited. I even find I listen in a different way in those circumstances. More than that, such meetings often prompt follow-on discussions at home in which things are said to parents for the first time and parents listen differently. The child psychologist William Yule found this when he was endeavouring to help girls who survived the sinking of the Jupiter. He stressed that by seeing and listening with parents and pupils initially in separate groups and then together, they were able 'to share publicly some of their feelings', and he added, significantly, 'Hopefully, that gave permission for such discussions to take place more readily at home' (Yule, 1989, p.5).

Not all such meetings will be with the tutor for a variety of reasons, partly time and partly because a hierarchy of listening adults is needed so that some meetings are with more senior staff whom the pupil meets less often and therefore less routinely. Thus the tutor must be part of a team. The usual arrangement is for a group of tutors if one year or adjacent years are to be coordinated and led by a more senior head of year or head of section. These roles are equally of importance to a school's ability to listen to children as that of tutors.

This team-leader role is one of the most difficult in schools, and probably the least well-defined, prepared for and analysed. The tradition has been for the year head to be more a 'super tutor' than a team-leader: she or he would see the 'difficult' children, taking over rather than enabling. The year head's role is central to a listening school. He or she both enables the tutors, and leads and demonstrates as an example. The post-holder has to ensure a good tutorial job description, induction and professional development, tutorial resources, monitoring, and referral of pupils. Typically the post-holder has insufficient opportunity to brief, induct, monitor and feed back.

In the other direction, the year head has to be part of a cohesive middle-management pastoral team clearly led by a senior, perhaps a deputy head. Again, the leadership is less common than it ought to be. Deputy heads can so easily be caught up with the urgent and short-term, with little time, still less secretarial support, and a heavy range of duties – especially coping with emergencies. When to influence the middle-management role and delivery substantially, when to take up a case personally, and when to support a year head by further training are key but difficult questions.

Heads, deputies, year heads and tutors all have to listen to pupils: when one and when another; and in what form reporting back, record-keeping and follow-up work is undertaken are amongst the sharpest questions in educational administration.

Counsellors

The team obviously should also include visiting or external counsellors. Ideally the staff of a large school would contain some specialised counselling time. Funding rarely allows this, although some schools have visiting counsellors who are on the staff of other organisations. The advantages include the students' ability to discuss matters with someone who is not a school authority figure or involved in any other aspect of their life: the counsellor would bring specific training and the experience of listening to a wide range of students; the session would be bookable and less likely to be curtailed or interrupted. Further, the counsellor would be available to advise teachers when they wished to discuss their work with a student. Such a counsellor cannot sort out all of a student's life's difficulties, but successful interventions are often possible through a series of, say, five 50-minute sessions.

All the staff are of course part of the same team, but from every pupil and family there has to be a clear network, with the possibility of referral. One function of team building is to support the individual members of staff in carrying the stress. The emotional burden of sensitive listening can be very great, and it is often too much for an individual. Teamwork is necessary for teachers. As Peter Maher (1987, p.199) says of child abuse: 'Teachers, like other professionals, need the opportunity to share their feelings, experiences, and thoughts with colleagues'.

Small-group reviews, in which individual members of staff share outlines of their actions, analysis and reactions, are both illuminating and supportive.

Curriculum content

You can listen only to what is said, and a well coordinated school includes in its curriculum the content to enable further retrospection, analysis and expression. You cannot teach what to think, of course, but the curriculum can facilitate thinking. Similarly, there would be no wish to have a standard way of saying what you feel and think, but expression can be better developed by teaching the appropriate language skills. Thus the attitudes, concepts and skills of the whole curriculum need to be checked against the pastoral need.

Self-analysis is necessary for communication and requires an especial skill – experience is insufficient. As Montaigne wrote in the sixteenth century:

> Whatever fruit we may glean from experience, that which we draw from outside experience will hardly contribute much even to our elementary education, unless we profit from the experience we can have of ourselves (Screech, 1983, p.101).

Thus, the curriculum must include some of the analytic concepts and their terminology to assist this 'experience of ourselves'. From quite early years self-reflection can be taught. For instance, a Year Nine course on parenting is part of a background understanding of how people work, and the use of a suitable set of questions and descriptive meaning will prompt fresh insights by the pupils. The study of photographs of facial expressions will prompt perceptions about feelings.

The question of the language curriculum is very important. Many adults see the teaching of grammar as the need for conventionally correct presentation rather than its deeper function of facilitating the thinking itself. For instance, relationships between facts is at the core of much grammar. In self-analysis and expression, verb tenses are a help to thinking out what you really did or experienced.

The paucity of the vocabulary of most British people is a national shame, and contributes to communication difficulties. The language curriculum should help vocabulary growth so that spelling is not a mere written politeness, but a way into understanding meaning. Too many pupils cannot express themselves because they do not have the words with which to do so.

Tone is another aspect that needs a specific approach. We tell off a child for using a wrong word, but less often do we teach about the aspect of meaning embodied in vocabulary choice. For instance, how do words gather a tone, and what is 'bad language'?

Such an approach to the language curriculum would help both the expression of pupils needing to be listened to now and better prepare them for the range of communication challenges of adult life. The research evidence on the high incidence of communication breakdown is depressing. In *The Cost of Communication Breakdown*, Janet Walker has shown that in such major human problems as child delinquency and marital breakdown, communication failure is a major cause, leading to 'a severe deterioration in the quality of life for children, parents, and the elderly' (Walker, 1995, p.4). Including self-understanding and verbal expression in the curriculum helps children be listened to *now* and prepares them for their adult responsibilities. The listening is enhanced by an appropriate pastoral and language curriculum.

Conclusion

Thus the school's overall planning includes its curriculum, pastoral care and staffing structure to facilitate the key trilogy of self-analysis, expression and listening. As John Dewey put it at the start of the twentieth century: 'There is all the difference in the world between having something to say and having to say something' (Dewey, 1900, p.57). We can help the pupils better toward 'having something to say' by ensuring they are listened to.

CHAPTER 6

Teachers and Pupils Listening to Each Other

Teifion Griffiths

> *Let your Scholer be never afraide, to aske you any dout, but use discretlie the best allurementes ye can, to encorage him to the same: lest, his overmoch fearinge of you, drive him to seeke some misorderlie shifte: as, to seeke to be helped by some other booke, or to be prompted by some other Scholer, and so goe aboute to begile you moch, and him selfe more.*
>
> *(The Scholemaster, 1570)*

These words of advice by Roger Ascham, tutor to the young Elizabeth were intended for teachers of Greek and Latin. Couched as they are in the highly wrought and carefully balanced words of the finest Elizabethan prose, they still seem strikingly apposite for many of us today. The first part of the quotation stresses the need for active participation of a good teacher in the encouragement of the pupil to be bold in his questioning and identifies Ascham as an active listener involved in a two-way, creative process. The second part, warning of what is likely to go wrong if this process is not encouraged, seems also to be equally relevant and to identify one of the major problems we face, both in school and society at large, namely the alienation that accompanies or arises from the lack of honest dialogue between children and parents or pupils and teachers.

Clearly Ascham would have had a much freer hand as a tutor than most schoolmasters would have enjoyed, but throughout his work he stresses the need for listening, persuading and gentleness in an age where 'overmoch fearinge' was regarded as a laudable part of education. In this, the second Elizabethan age, one can still detect in some quarters a sneaking regard for this, the draconian approach!

Modern schools are very busy places where a variety of activities, both planned and unplanned, take place for different pupils and teachers concurrently. It has been recognised that the hectic activity of schools combined with the number of pupils and staff involved, creates situations where listening to children might sometimes take a low priority. If it was ever thus, how much has the problem been exacerbated in recent years by new government legislation: the development of the National Curriculum, with a consequent increase in the number of subjects each pupil studies, the number of examinations sat, the amount of course-work to be completed, the INSET teachers have to attend, and the increase in work-load generally?

An *ad hoc* approach to encouraging and developing the position of listening as an important part of education would allow far too many pupils to 'escape the net'. Those with parents able to develop this would already be given the encouragement which sound listening provides; others have little access to adults with the time and inclination to listen to them. It is quite possible in a large comprehensive school for a pupil to avoid meaningful individual contact with an adult if he/she is inclined or even determined to do so. We need, therefore, to create and manage systems which make this unlikely to happen.

Children, like all of us, need to develop the ability to assess and reassess their position in relation to the world of parents, siblings, friends, teachers and other adults. They need to be able to tell and retell their own 'story'. Their own experiences form the essential basis for developing their skills of expression, which in turn appears to be a vital ingredient in reaching a level of informed decision-making. It is not enough, although many parents appear to fall for this fallacy, for children and adolescents to learn from each other! What they 'learn' may easily be chaotic or erroneous.

As far back as 1977, Lynn and Peel demonstrated that pupils 'require the help of teachers to benefit from informal discussion; it cannot be assumed that they benefit from a free situation'. Peel's work at Birmingham and that of his numerous postgraduate students was largely concerned with adolescent thinking and judgement, and based on classroom work covering a wide range of subjects.

One common problem in 'pastoral care' organisations in schools is that the carers become too readily involved in disciplinary and administrative activities. They spend too much time reacting to crises and become bogged down in paperwork. In such circumstances managements have distinct problems in setting up systems which may encourage teachers (and through them pupils) to participate in active and constructive listening.

Recent developments, including the National Curriculum, allow the learning process itself to become a focal point for this. OHMCI and OFSTED inspectors, in their evaluation and monitoring of classroom teaching, emphasise 'competence in key language skills, communicating ideas and information' as part of good learning and achievement; neither of these can take place without being underpinned by the ability to listen, by both pupil and teacher.

A perusal of the OHMCI *Handbook for the Inspection of Schools* (1994a) yields some of the following statements from those sections concerned with evaluation of standards, both of learning and teaching:

- good practice is identified where children display 'their ability to talk and listen in a variety of contexts' (p.50)
- 'listen to others and respond appropriately to what they say' (p.7)
- '... they listen sensitively and critically' (p.51)
- 'where standards are good pupils speak clearly and with increasing confidence; they communicate information effectively and give and respond to instructions appropriately and they listen purposefully and confidently engage in role-play and drama. Increasingly they sustain discussion and advocate and justify points of view' (p.50)
- '... establish use of mathematical language giving high priority to talk about work' (p.57)
- ' ... willing to listen to opinions which they may not share' (p.12)
- 'reading, reflection and discussion' (p.77)
- 'effective interaction' (p.42)
- 'pupils ... show a capacity to reflect on the experiences of life'(p.11)
- 'they are able to discuss their own and other people's beliefs' (p.11).

By including writing, listening and speaking among the key skills in all areas of the curriculum, HMI has given central importance to their progressive development throughout the child's school career. Other legislation, e.g. The Children Act 1989, actually demands that a child be listened to: as well as considering his physical, emotional and educational needs the court must take into account 'the ascertainable wishes and feelings of the child concerned (considered in the light of his age and understanding)'. Headteachers also have a duty to see that the spiritual development of their pupils is maintained.

The above examples give us some leverage in curriculum terms to encourage the notion of listening as an integral part of learning – even although this runs counter to the political situation where government ministers and even a chief inspector inveigh against child-centred, 'trendy' education and demand a return to 'traditional education', whatever that may be (OFSTED, 1995b).

In our first project into classroom observations at this school (some years ago), we concentrated wholly on two-way communication between teachers and pupils. Recent visits and observations required by appraisal and continuing evaluation by groups of senior staff show that this is an area in which we still need to make improvements. Sensitive and skilful questioning, in the hands of good practitioners, shows how we need to listen in order to encourage pupils to talk. This active listening elicits more mature and extended answers and clearly helps the pupil to clarify and develop not only skills of expression but also a sharper focus on the topic in hand, as well as intuitive thinking.

Encouraging teachers to develop their own listening skills, in classroom, group and individual activities, must be an essential part of departmental and school INSET, so that 'listening' becomes embedded in a whole-school approach to learning throughout the curriculum and the year groups. This can be encouraged by the pastoral curriculum as it operates through form registration and tutor periods. With the overcrowding of the curriculum as a result of the National Curriculum, some schools, especially in the primary section, require up to 120 per cent of available curriculum time just to cover the essential requirements of the curriculum orders. As a result, many schools were forced to abandon the weekly tutorial lesson and attempt to transfer issues which were previously in the pastoral curriculum into other subjects or cross-curricular areas. While this may have been possible in terms of dealing with 'areas covered' it has, unfortunately, led to a loss of time for listening which in many schools was such a feature of the tutorial period. At this school the introduction of active tutorial work had been such a successful initiative ten years ago that we made other curriculum accommodation to ensure its survival.

Central to a school's plan to provide appropriate systems to encompass opportunities for listening are:

1. The development of a sound pastoral system which has the support of pupils and staff.
2. A system to facilitate the effective delivery of the curriculum (for example, heads of school and heads of year liaising with heads of departments with this in mind).
3. A departmental or faculty system which works harmoniously with the above and is closely interwoven into it.
4. A sensitive system of monitoring and evaluation of standards, not only of academic and examination performance but also of the use made of listening and speaking in developing the pupil's abilities in all subject areas, including, of course, PSE.

5. All pupils, including those with special needs, being seen as the responsibility of the whole school.
6. PSE being given a regular place on the timetable in addition to registration/administration periods.
7. Extra-curricular/extra school activities receiving encouragement, ranging from school clubs and cultural events to residential experience and exchanges with schools abroad.
8. The school and its teachers accepting that they can make a difference to the child – i.e., the school should be child-focused.
9. Access to the whole curriculum, with support where necessary, for *all* pupils.

All these depend on the last element of the 'plan' which serves all the others, namely:

10. Development and training, which promote the above, are the right of all staff; to which end attendance at LEA INSET is actively encouraged and time and finance is made available for staff who wish to study for advanced diplomas and higher degrees.

Of the above, some are overtly and directly associated with listening or developing the associated capacities of rethinking, reworking and revising judgements, while others offer opportunities for listening to pupils as part of a larger strategy. For example, opportunities to engage in extra-curricular activities are of great importance to children with special needs (Short, 1993). We are aware of the great opportunities such activities offer for high-quality contact with pupils outside the school's traditional institutional constraints, but also know that SEN pupils, particularly those with physical disabilities, have often been excluded from them in the past. Parents are particularly supportive when a more adventurous stance is adopted.

It is wise for all aspects of the school's 'plan for listening' listed to be endorsed by the school's governors formally in their aims and objectives.

There are numerous examples of schools adopting what we could describe generally as a child-focused system. Keegan (1994) describes the effects of moving from a 'staff-centred organisation to one which is pupil-centred'; she regarded, when listening to her children, 'every complaint as an opportunity for improvement'. This strikes an affirmative and positive note. In a short period she has been able to demonstrate considerable improvements in a number of areas, including examination performance.

In the report of the same conference at which Keegan presented her paper, (OHMCI, Wales, 1994b) groups of headteachers, inspectors and advisers, in discussing 'the way forward', recorded,

> the pupil and not the parent should be viewed as the 'customer' in the new order of education ... schools need to create devices to promote pupil self-confidence [and, significantly] ... by talking to the children and examining exercise books it was possible to learn a great deal about the quality of teaching and learning and consequently produce an improvement. (p.25).

It is a truism that a satisfied customer is one who is listened to. In schools the curriculum itself provides regular and structured opportunities for pupils to consider, with adult help, their own experiences and to be taught to examine them critically and to express their own views about them. (Cooper, 1993a, p.157) points out that the,

> curriculum provides many practical opportunities for pupils to discover, explore and express their own views. Modular and coursework assignments offer pupils opportunities to pursue their own interests and lend themselves to interactive teacher styles, which encourage pupils' active participation in lessons.

This stresses also the pupil's 'universal right to be heard'.

The major problems which many comprehensive schools faced in their early days appeared to arise from the very powerful traditions of the old grammar schools. This 'contextual feature', as described in one case by Cooper (1993b), led to the situations where 'many pupils were faced with a curriculum that emphasised the weaknesses they had exhibited in order to fail to qualify for a grammar school place'. Similarly Bernstein (1973) posited that 'delicate overt and covert streaming arrangments' lower expectations dramatically. In such circumstances many schools, in order to address what they saw as a substantial problem of disenchantment, sought new ways of organisation, often by introducing mixed-ability groups and consequently opening access to the whole curriculum.

This situation was also evident at our school and many pupils expressed both openly and by their behaviour, concerns that they were missing out in their life-chances. Taking this on board meant acting to change school organisations by abolishing streaming and setting, broadening the curriculum and creating a listening pastoral system. In order to encourage acceptance of such change in a stable staff with a low turn-over, the cornerstone of the new structure had to be staff development and training.

A number immediately grasped the opportunity. It was felt that while *in situ* training, by offering new roles and role-shadowing for on-the-job experience, was important, it was also vital that they were offered the opportunity to mix with similarly-minded teachers from other schools in order to expand their horizons. This was possible because fortunately, in our geographical position, we had access to a number of universities and colleges which offered, in their education and management departments, suitable advanced diploma and Masters degree courses.

The first tranche were encouraged to follow courses which had a component concerned either with counselling or educational and behavioural difficulties. Whilst one objective was to improve staff qualifications, another, perhaps more important, was to help change the school's environment: essentially to turn it into a listening school. Of 80 or so staff employed over a period of 15 years, approximately 50 have taken advantage of this scheme. Time was given for some of the courses to be followed during the school day; these were largely funded by the LEA and more recently from the INSET and the LMS budget.

A curious bonus in a school which was poorly staffed was that many staff were both pastoral heads and heads of department; there was no alternative. It did, however, from the oustet break down the pastoral/academic divide and helped towards a cohesive approach. A number of Diploma and Masters dissertations, with the school acting as a client, concentrated upon the school's needs, addressing agreed subjects and providing carefully documented information and ideas to move us forward. They embraced such topics as Introducing Active Tutorial Work (one in Upper, the other in Lower School), Evaluation of Support Teaching, Sixth Form Choices, Communication within the school, The Introduction of an IT Policy, The Monitoring and Evaluation of Special Needs, and A Positive Reward System, as well as subject-based research.

Accompanying this activity came an increase in higher grade examination passes, including a 100 per cent improvement in pupils gaining five or more A – C grades. The change in philosophy has also meant that there have been no long-term exclusions or suspensions. It is also important, however, to note that there has been a huge increase in the numbers of staff now involved in pastoral work. An intensive system includes three heads of school, two assistant heads of sixth form, five heads of year and their deputies and a crucial role in the active tutorial work for almost 40 form tutors. In addition there are three careers staff and a head of GNVQ, all of whom are actively involved in offering advice and responding to pupils' vocational needs.

Careers advice and provision of work experience offer excellent scope for constructive listening and building relationships with all pupils. A particularly successful method relating to work experience, both in Year

10 and the sixth form, involves a team approach. Volunteer staff take responsibility for the work placement of five or six pupils each. This gives a personal feel to the exercise and includes several initial meetings about choice of placement, visiting the pupil at work and debriefing them later. There is also a whole-staff report-back session involving up to 40 staff.

More recently, forms of mentoring have been introduced, particularly for newcomers into the sixth form (Year 10). This is now being extended, by staff request, to individual pupils in other years, in order to help those we feel are being stressed by the demands of the National Curriculum, and especially those in Years 10 and 11, who, while not presenting the more obvious symptoms of disaffection, are identified as having problems with organising their work, especially coping with the demands of course work. We are currently examining the possibility of a mentoring system for the next Year 7 intake.

Further developments also lend themselves to active listening on the part of the head of year and tutors. Careers and options advice has recently been aided by the introduction of careers conferences, specifically for Year 9. Another recent, and at first not universally welcomed, turn of events has been a growing number of pupils accompanying their parents to school parents' evenings. Some teachers find this a welcome opportunity to persuade parents to listen to their children! In liaison with feeder schools we now arrange for the head of first year and deputy to visit all feeder primaries (over 30) and spend time with next year's newcomers. In addition, pupils and parents visit the school together in the summer term, pupils spend a day on timetable, and very early in the autumn term, an informal evening is held at the school with refreshments and disco. At this particular evening it is possible for individual problems to be raised and the foundation for good relationships to be laid.

All the above provide wide–ranging opportunities for pupils to be given one-to-one opportunities to raise issues with staff and are intended to encourage meaningful communication where the student's voice can be heard. Most of what has so far been described shows that a school can produce a wealth of opportunity to listen to and to hear its pupils views. A more formal development currently taking off is the establishment of a school council. For several years there has been a sixth form council headed by a head boy and head girl elected by the students. The extension of such a council into the rest of the school will, it is hoped, allow pupils' voices to inform further school development.

The positive elements in the National Curriculum and the Guidelines for Inspection (particularly their highlighting of listening as a Key Skill), have up to a point allowed us to use the curriculum to our advantage. In primary schools, while the evaluating and assessment procedures have had to be streamlined considerably, the impact of the National Curriculum is controversial. Some teachers see it as legitimising established traditions of classroom and curriculum organisation. Others, such as Alexander (1992) and the so-called 'Three Wise Men' envisage radical changes, with more emphasis on subject teaching and ability grouping (Alexander *et al.*, 1992). The fact that many primary teachers still take their class for most of the week means that they are able to engineer, in the normal course of events, regular and frequent occasions for listening to individual pupils. Often the day begins with some form of listening, 'on the mat' exercise. The majority of children of primary age are willing, often eager, to share their story with the teacher and classmates. The relatively small size of the schools also means that distressed or unhappy children are more easily identifiable. The more flexible use of time in primary classes removes some of the constraints present in the secondary school. A significant part of their time is still taken up in developing communication skills, including listening, which makes them central to the whole primary experience. At this stage also there is usually still a close involvement with parents, and staff are readily available to discuss problems with them. To some degree primary schools are always in advance of secondary, having felt the rigours of the NC and SATS before us. It remains to be seen whether they will be able to retain their commitment to such fundamental principles of post-Plowden practice as the generalist class teacher and to learning through topics.

From what has been written above, one could be excused for assuming that the many constructive ways in which schools have accommodated the welter of new legislation which began in what now seem the far-off and gentle days of Keith Joseph's period of office, and have accelerated so wildly in recent times, have left us with a feeling of optimism, yet an awful ambivalence casts its shadow over the many positive achievements. Clearly many good things have been accomplished but there are growing concerns which many share, largely caused by the lack of genuine consultation with schools and teachers in the construction of policy and the great stresses placed upon pupils and parents in the relentless pursuit of academic success and the down-grading of other skills and achievements. In such a situation it is clear that some of us are not being listened to ourselves!

Major barriers are being placed in the way of our attempts to be listening schools. The five-year moratorium promised by Dearing shows little chance of being honoured.

While aiming for 'breadth and balance', the spread of the academic curriculum puts other activities, including listening, under threat. There is no doubt that many pupils are suffering under increased pressure to an extent that extra mentoring and counselling may fail to offset it. Should this lead to increased alienation and disenchantment, a major casualty would be the school's pastoral work. One fears that more and more pastoral heads would have to revert to being almost wholly purveyors of authority or discipline, and their roles as listeners in a constructive relationship with pupils would become untenable (cf Galloway, 1990).

Sweetingham and Woods (1994) point out that there are clearly perceived 'risks of self-exposure and possible rejection' involved in disclosing problems to other people, especially to those in an authority role. This particularly affects the need for 'empathetic listening and counselling skills', central to the interventionist role which most of our pastoral staff would want to employ. One already sees evidence of breakdown in some parent/child relationships; a growing number of pupils are apparently rejected by their parents and we witness increasing numbers of children from Year 9 onwards being placed in care and older pupils living alone in temporary accommodation.

Nevertheless, Kyriacou and Butcher (1993) show that the main stresses upon Year 11 children are still academic, largely to do with examinations and meeting deadlines for assessed work. Non-academic concerns are identified as bullying, health, money and family disagreements.

A central irony of our present situation is that caused by the ambivalent, conflicting messages we have been receiving from central government, successive Secretaries of State and the HMI. Peagram and Upton (1991) highlight a particular irony in their examination of the Elton report:

> ... most of the recommended changes are ones of attitude and classroom and within-school organisation and related to teachers, parents, pupils and LEAs. This is interesting when viewed in comparison to most other areas of education where central government has been exercising increasingly detailed control over school organisation and curriculum, both directly through the powers of the Secretary of State, and indirectly by promulgating effectiveness criteria which reflect a preoccupation with academic as opposed to social outcomes. (p. 42.3).

This neatly describes what may lead to diminishing the effectiveness of the many caring and listening institutions which have grown during the 'ascendancy' of the comprehensive ideal. Attacks emerge from those right-wing pressure groups in the grim tradition of the Black Paper writers of the 1960s, (e.g., Cox and Boyson, 1977) and are clearly impressing some government politicians who ignore official figures, which, even by their own 'academic' standards, show considerable success, for example the improvement in the number of pupils gaining at least five GCSEs at Grades A – C. This appears to be part of a systematic attempt to downgrade teachers in the eyes of the public and destroy their credibility. It occasionally leads to comical interludes, almost in Monty Python style, as when, in 1992, a government minister one day announced the great success of the GCSE examination results only to be followed very shortly afterwards by the Secretary of State spuriously using part of an HMI report to query the examinations' validity. The press reported this widely, and there was obvious distress and confusion in the minds of many parents and candidates (vide *The Guardian*, 27 August 1992 and *The Observer*, 6 September 1992).

Another group of 'barriers' to listening arises directly from the series of financial cuts which LEAs have recently borne: it is, unfortunately, work at local centres and the use of outside help which has virtually disappeared in some areas. This was of particular importance in helping children with behavioural difficulties. It is sometimes vital to have an additional adult, not directly involved with the school, who is able to provide unthreatening listening and make objective evaluations which, in some fraught circumstances, the school might find difficult to provide.

Other stringencies affect the INSET programme and there have been substantial increases in fees for courses in higher education. As this provision has been the basis of our developments, it must be continued as far as possible unless we are to revert to the insular position we inherited. An intensive commitment to this kind of training is becoming more difficult and so skills of counselling, and the benefits of mixing with other professionals and sharing their knowledge and experience, may be forfeited.

Many of the LEA INSET courses have been organised by LEA advisers, including those in pastoral care and counselling. As finance disappears, advisory teams are forced to finance themselves through operating inspection teams – they are therefore not always available to perform their original advisory role. Where they are available, the tendency is for them to be forced, by NC demands and government pressures, to become more narrowly subject-based, supplying the immediate demand and neglecting pastoral and cross-curricular areas. This also affects badly some of the joint enterprises which have been run in some authorities with organisations such as NAPCE.

Most serious of all, because its effects are legion, is the pressure which financial constraints make on staffing. While most governing bodies make staffing a top priority, there is a limit, when budgets shrink, on the number of teachers they can employ. This of course was behind the current unrest among many governors in 1995 who threatened to produce deficit budgets. Particularly vulnerable in this situation are those intermediate pastoral heads who Marland (1974) identified as so important in 'imprinting house or year in a pupils' understanding'. Those positions often give young members of staff an opportunity to gain valuable experience. Often their diligence commended them to the staff, but above all they proved a success with pupils.

In spite of the suspicions, often unfounded, which are regularly released in the right-wing press, about mixed-ability teaching, many of us who have introduced it have found it a positive boon, producing in addition to a more civilised atmosphere, a greater possibility to provide for entitlement and a more economical management of teaching time. The ill-advised move to introduce the starred 'A' grade at GCSE and the consequent espousal of tiered examination papers, may, more than anything else, undermine much of the progress we have made. These papers, allowing the achievement of a limited number of grades, may discourage schools from entering pupils at the higher levels. If we couple with this the insistence on the production of crude league tables we can envisage a return to the sort of academic pressure which attacks the whole basis of the listening school.

The genuine progress which has been made over several years is now under threat. The government still sees schools as civilising agents but, by a misguided insistence on traditional methodology and 'chalk and talk', does not allow us to practise those very skills which we have developed and which, ironically, would be likely to produce what they require. Our leaders themselves display a frightening inability to listen. We have provided an increase in academic standards; indeed genuine pastoral care demands this as much as anything. Recent changes may lead to the destruction of listening and the consequence will be an increase in apathy and disaffection. The Thompson Report (DES, 1982) on the Youth Service in England, showed the alarming extent of this problem. Three-quarters of the youth in the survey were 'politically apathetic'. The Archbishop of Canterbury's (1985) Commission on Urban Priortiy Areas, concluded that 'extremist groups ... work aggressively to take advantage of young people and gain their allegiance', and stressed that it was 'impossible to overstress the seriousness of this situation'. It also found that 'education even in comprehensive schools continues to be highly selective, competitive and cerebral'.

Unless we are to preside over a series of lost opportunities it behoves us to make what stand we can against current directions. We need to be vigilant and fight for the flexibility which a pupil-centred education demands; insisting upon examinations which affirm success rather than record failure, and, where we identify successful practice, to strive to maintain it. Through the press and our associations or unions we need to be constantly questioning what are becoming the sacred cows of a new educational establishment of the right. The overweaning influence of its pressure groups must be exposed for what it is: a doctrinaire attempt to undermine good practice in a system intended to benefit all our pupils.

We need also, crucially, to fight to retain an objective inspectorate and highlight and oppose the role played by those who are obviously political appointments chosen for their partisan stance rather than their educational objectivity. If we stand squarely against this then the listening school may yet survive.

CHAPTER 7

Listening to Children in Schools: An Empirical Study

Marion Bennathan

Introduction

The Education Reform Act of 1988 was radical legislation, intended to bring about great changes in schools. A National Curriculum, statutory measurement of progress, publication of results, greater involvement of parents, parental choice of schools, all these challenged accepted practice, provoked heated debate and started a process of profound change in the educational climate, which continues. The Act set out to 'promote the spiritual, moral, cultural, mental and physical development of pupils at school and in society'. It also aimed to 'prepare pupils for the opportunities, responsibilities and experiences of adult life'.

This last led many of us to expect that the idea of involving young people in decisions about their life in school would have a central part of the Act, but that did not happen. This is in strong contrast to the Children Act which was in preparation at the same time and which became law the following year. In this, consultation with children and their involvement in decisions to be taken about them is a constantly recurring theme.

Legislation about children and young people reflects, implicitly or explicitly, the views held about the formative influences in their lives. Those in child care, in child psychology and psychiatry, have changed profoundly in the professional lifetime of many of us. It is now taken as evident that children have a perception of what is happening to them which helps to structure their response, their behaviour. From this it follows that if we wish to promote their good development we must understand the child's point of view. If their perceptions are negative, perhaps distorted as a result of bad experiences, we must put in work and resources to change them. The wide acceptance of this reality has changed practice in much work with children and it is what underlies the emphasis of the 1989 Children Act on involving children in decisions about their lives.

The child's point of view

Great harm can be done to children by well-meaning adults who fail to understand how the child interprets what is happening. It was, for example, standard practice until the late 1950s not to allow parents to visit small children in hospital. The reasoning was that the parents' departure would distress the child and perhaps retard its recovery. The work of Bowlby (1953) showed that very small children could interpret their parents' absence as rejection or punishment. They might feel that they had been abandoned for ever. Depression, withdrawal or extreme anger might be the result, and if the separation were prolonged or the return home badly managed, permanent emotional damage might result.

Children in the care of local authorities or of reputable charities were, as late as the 1960s, exported to Canada, Australia and other British possessions in a philantrophic movement which started in the 1870s. The laudable aim was to give young people from poverty-stricken backgrounds a chance of a better life. For many of them this was a disaster. Often sent without the knowledge of their families, their records lost, some were ill-treated, abused and exploited. The effect on their emotional development and their adult lives was frequently disastrous. The efforts of some of them to regain contact with their origins led in 1987 to the founding of the Child Migrants Trust, whose work has been given wide media attention and is described movingly by Bean and Melville (1989) in *Lost Children of the Empire*, and Humphreys (1994) in *Empty Cradles*.

Practice in child care had changed radically for reasons now widely understood. Rowe (1982), writing for adoptive parents, put the matter clearly:

> Even in ordinary families, without the changes and upsets which occur in adoption, much of the adult world is confusing to a young child. ... When there has been no order in a child's life he cannot begin to make sense of it and, since many unpleasant things seem to have happened as punishment for his naughtiness, the little child tends to assume that all painful events are the result of his badness. ...According to circumstances and temperament, some children will take this inwardly with withdrawn behaviour and nervous symptoms, while others react with anger and aggression. Both sorts of behaviour are the child's way of warding off painful feelings of anxiety and

guilt. They can only be given up as the child is helped to understand what is happening and why.

Relevance to education

If it is now accepted in most areas of work with children that understanding their perception is essential to understanding their response, why was this principle not enshrined in the 1988 Education Act? Why were legislators apparently not aware of these changes in our understanding of children (Davie, 1994)? Surely the idea of the child as a passive recipient of services has had its day. Children have to be understood as interactive, as having a self-concept, an identity, which shapes their view of what is offered to them, in school as elsewhere, and which therefore must be taken into account as routinely by their teachers as it is by other professional groups.

Experience in special education

One group of educators has for a long time been aware that their pupils come to them with extremely negative perceptions of adults and of education. Workers with the maladjusted, now called 'pupils with emotional and behavioural difficulties', take it for granted that pupils have to have their point of view understood and respected if they are going to develop more positive attitudes. Moreover, many of the pioneers in residential work with such young people thought that the best way to break down the hostility and poor self-esteem from which they commonly suffered was to give them responsibility in helping to run the school. David Wills at Bodenham Manor, Otto Shaw at Red Hill, and AS Neill at Summerhill, for example, all made it a central part of their philosophy (Bridgeland,1971). As Laslett (1995) writes, many such schools,

> adopted processes which involved children in sharing with adults in the running of the school, or taking responsibility for some parts of its organisation. There were sound reasons for doing this. It was an obvious illustration of the staff's intention to counter children's belief that staff were on one side and they were on another. It prevented children from believing that the staff did things *to* them by giving evidence that they did things *with* them. It was evidence that the staff regarded the children, that they trusted them and took their views seriously when decisions affecting them were discussed. It provided children with a valuable contradictory experience of adults: they did not treat them and their opinions as many adults had treated

> them in the past when decisions about them were made without any reference to them. Being given responsibility for some parts of the school organisation or activities altered children's perceptions of themselves. It gave them a feeling of worth and this, too, contradicted previous feelings about themselves.

Pupils in mainstream schools

It would be far from the truth to suggest that the idea of pupil involvement is not already well established in much work on mainstream education. Two examples: Rutter *et al.* (1979) in their influential *Fifteen Thousand Hours*, which looked for the factors which made some schools more successful than others over a wide range of criteria, noted that 'crucial influences will include.... shared activities between staff and pupils, (and) pupil positions of responsibility within the school system' (p.194). Second, in 1984, David Hargreaves, summarising the findings of an extensive survey of the views of secondary school pupils in the Inner London Education Authority on their experience of school, wrote:

> Pupils experience school as a totality and they need to feel and to be involved in all areas of it, and not merely in isolated and trivial matters....A cause of disaffection amongst some pupils is their gradually accumulated conviction that they have no real voice in matters of school policies and decision-making pertaining to the curriculum, distribution of resources, the physical environment, and rules and sanctions (para 3.12.1).

He found that even the experience of being consulted for the purposes of the survey had improved pupils' attitudes and concluded that a shift was urgently needed in the way that pupils are treated in the wider aspects of school life.

Thus before the consultative processes that preceded the 1988 Education Act, there was a growing body of evidence that many pupils would function better for being more involved in the running of their schools. This and the fact that this way of thinking about children was now accepted good practice in child care and in special education led to the question of why most mainstream schools were apparently not seen by legislators as ready to accept the principle of pupil consultation.

The present study

It was decided to carry out a brief enquiry to find examples of schools with a high level of pupil involvement and, if the results were encouraging, to give them publicity in the hope that this would contribute to the discussion of and lead to greater pupil involvement.

All LEAs in England were written to, explaining the purpose of the enquiry and asking if they could give examples of the sort of good practice which ought to be encouraged. From the replies, about 30 schools which seemed promising were chosen and their headteachers contacted by telephone.

None felt that their school was going so far as to build formal consultation with pupils into the school's constitution. Many of them felt that they could not give as much time as was desirable to involving pupils. Some had projects which they thought might be of interest but they were modest about them: no grand claims. Discussion would be welcome and several of the most easily accessible were visited. Six of the schools, one primary and the rest secondary, were particularly focused on consulting pupils and are reported on. While the enquiry was anything but exhaustive, the visits and the discussions with teachers and with pupils were interesting and seem worth sharing with a wider audience.

School A

This was a comprehensive school in a pleasant village, commuter territory for the nearby university town. The headteacher was three years in post, her second headship. When she arrived she had found a school with a good academic record for the majority of its pupils.

The main problem she saw was a sizeable group of disaffected 14- and 15-year-olds, mostly boys, who were getting considerable status among themselves from negative attitudes to work, and from vandalism in school and outside in the community. She thought that the way to change these attitudes was to involve pupils and staff in more effective, more consistent relationships. This meant changing the existing tutorial system. All staff were given a group of pupils across the school's age range, with whom they were to stay throughout the pupil's school career.

There was a daily tutorial period and considerable thought and staff training were given to how best to use this, not only or mainly for administrative tasks but for discussion and debate on all sorts of issues affecting life in school. There were structured discussions of such things as school rules, school meals and the physical care of the buildings. There were also activities to do with the personal development of each pupil. One teacher, interested in drama, used group techniques for relaxation and body control which pupils found useful for coping with stress, such as at examination times. Staff and pupils shared experiences across tutor groups of what was and was not found useful and enjoyable.

The head did not set out specifically to involve pupils in the management of the school but the closer relationships that developed between staff and pupils and the enthusiasm shown by the staff for the new tutorial system provided the natural setting for shared decision-taking. This began to take place at many levels. When, for example, candidates for teaching posts were shown round the school by pupils it became clear that the guides were quite astute observers of the guided. One of the senior staff who was particularly good at listening to pupils, 'a genius on the grapevine', gathered up impressions which were then taken into account in the final selection of staff.

Sometimes quite specific problems were put to the pupils. School meals, for example, had been much criticised. Choice was limited; quantities were inadequate; ingredients were not in line with pupils' growing awareness of healthy eating. The new school council, which consisted of a representative from each study group, devised a questionnaire, and gathered in and analysed the results. Having faced the problem of achieving some consensus of what was wanted, they then agreed that the delicate task of negotiating change with the catering staff was best left to the head.

The impression gained from sitting anonymously in the staffroom and from walking about the school with the head was of high morale and confident and purposeful activities. There were good relationships evident amongst staff and pupils and a lack of the tensions found in schools where discipline is a central issue. The head was clearly a familiar sight about the school, knew a great deal of what was going on, and was met with respect and friendliness wherever we went. She had decided and positive views on the sharing of authority amongst colleagues and pupils. This, she felt, was perfectly consistent with the principle that headteachers were there to manage and ultimately to be responsible to governors for carrying out agreed policies.

School B

This comprehensive school in a pleasant, small, commuter town, made contact to ask if their 'Day 11' scheme would be of interest to the enquiry, and so a visit was made to learn about it. 'Day 11' is so called because the school has a ten-day timetable which, once each half term, is suspended to allow all staff to offer some activity, in or out of school, which need have nothing to do with what they normally teach.

The range on offer was wide. There was, for example, orienteering; walking in the nearby hills; a day trip to Alton Towers; Welsh cooking; French cooking; boys' games for girls; snooker and squash; making comics; making cartoons. Pupils were given as free a choice as possible, almost aways getting their first or second choice. They were asked to pay any necessary costs, with a fund being discreetly available for those for whom this was difficult.

Evaluation by pupils was seen as an important part of the exercise, with all of them being asked to write up comments on their experience. At the top of the sheet were guidelines: 'Write something about each of the following: Fun. Value for money. Did you use the time well? What did you learn? Would you do this day again? If so, why? If not, why not?'

A random sample of the evaluations was seen which, it was said, were typical in being overwhelmingly positive but by no means uncritical, for example:

> BOYS' GAMES FOR GIRLS: This Day 11 was good but not as good as some I've done. Lots of girls came because they wanted a chance to play football, like me. But when we got to doing the skills it was not much use as we didn't use them in a game. Thank goodness we didn't have to go through the cricket skills. Quite an enjoyable day.

> COMICS AND CARTOONS: This activity was the best I've ever been on. It was fun and just generally brilliant. I did the best artistry I've ever done and it stimulated my thoughts. It was very interesting and good value and I would really like to do this again. Unfortunately, Darren didn't bring his ghetto-blaster so we couldn't sing the Space Marines Anthem, but I enjoyed it very much nevertheless.

Evaluations were collected by tutors and passed on to the teacher concerned by the senior teacher in charge of the project. We discussed the benefits of the project. Were they enough to justify the time it took? This had been considered in an extensive evaluation of the project by pupils, parents and staff who overwhelmingly favoured its continuance.

Staff and pupils independently noted that relationships changed for the better: 'Pupils apppreciate getting to know different staff and getting to know them in a different way'. Most teachers felt that the time taken was well-spent. They saw children in a different light, having been with them in new contexts. This change of attitude spilt over into the classroom and had a positive effect on work and discipline. Pupils recognised that they were being given real choices, and also saw their teachers in a different light as they discussed the pros and cons of each scheme in their tutor groups.

The senior teacher in charge acknowledged that there are issues of staff confidence, a theme which recurred in our discussion in other schools, but she felt that these diminished as experience grew. Some teachers initially felt that their popularity might be put to the test and shown to be wanting by the choices made by pupils. In fact, whether pupils were more interested in the activity on offer than in the teacher in charge of it, or whether some teachers underestimated their popularity, this had almost ceased to be a concern.

There was also apprehension about pupils' evaluations, again a recurring theme in our enquiries. In fact, almost always pupils were constructive in their criticisms and none had been offensive. The teacher in charge took care to feed the evaluations back privately to individual teachers, but this was because of teacher confidence, not because of their contents. The senior teacher felt that to introduce change, to persuade colleagues to try out the new experiences necessary for greater pupil participation in the life of the school, was a threat to many teachers. It therefore required considerable support and encouragement.

School C

When telephoned, the head said that he had no formal project for pupil participation but that he consulted pupils about the running of the school all the time.

In a most enjoyable visit to the large, four-storey 1960s comprehensive school in a pleasant seaside town, the atmosphere of trust and friendliness amongst staff and pupils shone out in a multitude of ways. The relaxed and cheerful conversation in the staffroom; the enthusiastic shop-talk; the pleasantly confident manner of the pupil who showed the way to the head's room – all proclaimed a school of high morale.

The head and several other teachers spoke with enthusiasm of the changed attitudes to pupils brought about by the recently introduced methods of assessment, the change from the end of year report compiled solely by staff to records of achievement which are agreed by staff and pupils. These highlighted areas where change was needed, areas of pupil weakness and strength. But they also gave the staff feedback, in a new way, about what pupils enjoyed learning and what they did not.

The head saw these changes as fundamental and exciting for the education system as a whole. He saw them as just as important in increasing pupil involvement as the move away from selection and streaming at the age of 11. The trend away from direction to negotiation, to choice and discussion, gives the pupil much more autonomy and changes the teacher's role from control to support and guidance. The whole staff found the changes exciting and positive, enhancing pupils' dignity and self-esteem.

Pressed to give specific examples of pupil participation in school management, the head was reluctant. He said that he would be worried if consultation were confined to a particular situation rather then being a way of life. He would not, for example, think of changing a school rule without extensive discussion with staff, pupils, parents and governors. He would not necessarily give the decision to pupils, who left to themselves are capable of being much more draconian than adults. But what pupils said would be listened to.

What was very apparent in this school were the positive qualities of the head, his visibility and approachability to staff and pupils, and his ability to manage and to lead.

School D

This was a comprehensive school in a large industrial city, in a suburb of less than average prosperity. The head was young, fairly new to the school, with clear ideas of the changes he wanted to achieve. On appointment he felt that the school was well-controlled with somewhat complacent staff. Pupils on entry were placed in streamed classes on the basis of their junior school group test results. These were overall below average, which the staff accepted as the cause of the school's rather poor academic standards.

The head felt that the involvement of pupils in management was not something to be considered in isolation but as part of a positive ethos. Schools had their own value systems, often implicit, and the staff had to look critically at the school culture.

To take the issue of streaming: group tests of ability may be unreliable. Pupils put in lower streams on this basis might thereby be labelled, and label themselves, as of low ability. The claim that there were opportunities for children to move, was in fact unreal. Pupils tended to perform as expected and so did not usually move out of a lower stream. Also, if one did, then another pupil must be moved down – a damaging process. So rigid streaming denied pupils the best chance of development.

There were other issues. For instance, gender: if girls in this mixed school felt that it was not feminine to be clever they would tend to underperform. Retardation: pupils with literacy problems could be harmed by well-meant treatment offered so insensitively as to add to their lack of self-esteem. Racial prejudice: in any school, not only one with a high proportion of pupils from ethnic minorities – all these important issues had to be acknowledged, discussed and addressed. First the staff had to define proactive policies which must then be transmitted urgently to pupils, so that they started expecting a great deal from their school. This explicit acceptance of shared values was the necessary background for involving pupils in the management of schools. In a school with unacceptable values, pupils given authority could become the agents of malpractice.

The head, therefore, with much staff time for consultation and visits to schools which were examples of good practice, began to make changes. First streaming was abolished. Then a tutorial system was introduced. Staff were given considerable time and extensive training for this. First year groups, for example, were presented with the sort of problems that might confront any first year pupil and asked for advice. What should someone do who had arrived at school without their packed lunch and with no money to buy a school dinner? What if a first year boy was being threatened or bullied by a fourth year boy? Pupils worked in groups, discussed and recorded their advice and then shared it with other groups. The tutor then joined the discussion and helped the group to a consensus or a truce.

Staff had come to see that what was achieved by this sort of approach was complex and valuable. The children, new to the school, were implicitly given the reassurance that the problems they might have to face were not unusual; that they and their peers were thought capable of contributing to a solution; that the adults in authority wanted and valued their views. In short, they learnt that they had a considerable part in the decision-making on the problems of life in school.

Positive involvement was also present in academic work. Pupils discusssed their progress in each subject with their teachers and set agreed targets for the next half term's work. When these targets were met, a letter of commendation was sent home to parents and a copy stored in a well-produced folder which went with the pupil through the school. These procedures, like the tutorial system, brought about contacts between teachers and pupils which were changing relationships. One effect of this was that teachers developed a much better understanding of what was causing blockages for each child. Group judgements of success and failure, as every teacher knew, tended to emphasise but not explain the failure. Without better understanding, the failure persisted and the child lost motivation. Unmotivated children were the bane of any teacher's life, taking time unproductively, not able or willing to get on with their agreed work, and likely to disturb others who would. By positive and regular involvement of pupils, children became confident that they could reveal their difficulties and get help, which reduced the anxiety that lay behind many school problems. Teachers got new ideas about effective teaching so that learning became more of a shared process. So often, said the head, we taught children without getting to know them well enough to make use of the knowledge and interest they brought to school.

To give pupils yet another share in school management, the head had started a school council. It was so far only for first year pupils with a delegate from each tutor group and would go up through the school with the present first year. The council was held in the dinner break with two teachers in attendance, whose brief was to be available but not to direct.

Problems to be tackled could come from council members or be referred to them by staff or other pupils. One such issue was what was to be done about pupils' dissatisfaction with the dinner break. Staffing levels did not allow for the supervision of classrooms and so the practice had been for the school to be locked. This caused many difficulties, especially in bad weather. The council recommended that some rooms in the Lower School should be accessible to first year pupils, with council members being responsible for their good care. They also recommended that their £50 grant should be spent on board games of their choosing to keep pupils enjoyably occupied.

The council met to demonstrate its working. First, the normal agenda: some of the board games had not been well cared for and pieces were missing. This dealt with, they moved on to the disco that had been organised for first year pupils. This was judged to have been a success and it was decided to hold another.

We then talked about the council and what it meant to members. After a little hesitation the talk was free and enthusiastic, both about the council and the school generally. One boy of Asian origin said that he had learnt to speak up in public in a way that surprised him and which he thought would be useful in his grown-up life. A voluble, lively girl said that working with teachers differently from other schools had helped her to understand what school was about, and what the difficulties were in running a school to help everybody. She said thoughtfully that when she had children of her own she would understand much better what she wanted them to get out of education.

One shy-seeming little girl eventually spoke. She said that she had never talked much at her junior school. After the meeting, the teachers said that there had been concern there at the level of her withdrawal. She had not understood that her teachers would be interested in what she had to say. Her friend, the talkative girl, had persuaded her to join the council and she felt much more comfortable about talking in public.

After the council, the two teachers present said that the children had surprised them by the speed with which they had grasped the rules of orderly discussion and decision-making. They themselves had had to learn the art of letting overt control go, and admitted to some initial difficulty in not taking charge. They felt that the council was proving successful on two counts. First, it had thought out practical solutions to quite serious problems, such as what to do about the potentially stressful dinner break. Second, it was helping children in their personal development. All the children were learning negotiating skills. Some of them had come to the school with considerable problems of self-management or behaviour. The quiet little girl was one example. Her talkative friend was another, having arrived in school with a reputation for poor concentration and a tendency to distract others with her chattering. She was becoming visibly more controlled and responsible as, they thought, she felt valued and listened to by the council. A boy who had been noticeably tense and wary, and who had only spoken when spoken to directly, had come up from the junior school with a reputation for being hostile and difficult. He had progressed significantly in self-confidence, worked most conscientiously at his dinner-time duties and seemed set to make much better progress.

To have other views on pupil participation, meetings were organised with other members of staff; the head of science can represent them. He had been at the school for several years, enjoyed teaching chemistry to his streamed classes and was not disposed to change. He liked the new head, was impressed by his attitude to staff and eventually, persuaded by his arguments, agreed to visit other schools where rigid streaming was not the practice. He was so impressed with what he saw that he willingly changed the system in his department. He also caught the spirit of pupil consultation, prepared a questionnaire and circulated it to all his classes, to be completed anonymously if they wished. This asked them to evaluate his lessons, to say what they liked and disliked and why, and to suggest changes. He thought that pupils had taken the task seriously. He was naturally pleased with the highly positive responses he got but inevitably there were differences of opinion. These he summarised and presented to the class who then had the valuable experience of achieving agreement about any changes needed.

His conclusion was that the time given to this exercise was time well spent. He thought that there had been a significant improvement in pupils' morale and commitment to the subject. After all, if a course of action had been agreed after extensive consultation, the teacher was sharing responsibility with the class and not relying solely on his own authority. Peer group pressure was a powerful tool and one often used against authority, particularly in the third and fourth year of secondary school. Pupil participation could enable this pressure to be used positively.

The head of science was a confident and experienced teacher, clearly enjoying his job. He thought that many were resistant to listening to pupils because of teacher confidence which had to be managed by senior staff if the level of threat was not to be unacceptable to some. This was an issue that came up in most of the schools we visited and one that therefore merited further investigation.

Before we leave this school, it is again important to stress the head's role in achieving change. Like the other two heads discusssed earlier, he was of high ability not only academically but in management skills. He had clear aims, well-presented and adequately discussed with his staff, and he had authority. Walking about the school with him, it was obvious that he was a frequent and welcome visitor to his staff and pupils. He knew what they were doing, he was interested and positive. He was well in touch. The skills of heads were clearly central to our search.

School E

All the schools discussed so far have been secondary schools. Contact was also made with some primary schools. School E is an infant school in an inner London borough and has a head who believes that no pupil is too young to be made to feel that she or he has ideas to contribute to the good running of the school.

The case of the school assembly demonstrates the point. The tradition was to have a mid-morning assembly, with children taking part, presenting their work, choosing the songs. Yet clearly the assembly was not working well. The children were restless, inattentive and bored. The head and her staff could have taken the decision to make changes, but instead she consulted the children, class by class. She found them well able to explain what they liked and what they did not like. First, some classes tended to arrive late because they had been engrossed in doing other things, so the other children had to wait, doing nothing, which was very unpopular. Then while children liked showing their work to each other, what children said could not always be heard and some went on too long. Then sometimes the head was cross with them about some school problem which they found quite uncomfortable in the big group.

They suggested changes. All classes must promise to be on time, and to help this a warning bell was rung. Then children presenting work had to learn to do so clearly and briefly. Work was then to be left on display so that children could look at it in their own time. If the head was unavoidably delayed, another teacher took her place and the meeting started on time. And when criticisms were necessary, the head spoke to classes individually.

Assemblies were now lively, successful events with a high level of participation and attention, and the children were regularly reminded that they had a voice in the running of the school.

Meeting teachers' anxieties

It will be clear that in the schools described so far, pupil participation was judged to be a resounding success. It was seen as improving motivation and morale, and lessening behaviour problems. And yet, in many schools, this valuable resource is largely untapped. Changing staff attitudes was identified in most of the schools visited as a central issue and a necessary step to achieving change, so a second visit was made to the sixth school to discuss teachers' resistance to greater pupil involvement.

School F

This was a girls' comprehensive school in a London borough with most of its pupils from ethnic minorities. On the first visit, most of the time had been spent with the headteacher who had been at the school for many years, having been appointed to introduce pastoral care when that was a new concept. The openness of communication and the supportive relationships between the Head and her staff was striking. This and a long tradition of pupil consultation made it seem a good place to discuss in greater depth teachers' attitudes to change.

The head talked of the threat that she thought many teachers experienced when asked to re-think their attitude to pupils. Teachers, particularly at secondary level but probably generally, were well taught to manage their subjects intellectually. Their professional self-respect had rested quite considerably on their ability to do this – to achieve good academic results. Their emotional security had rested on their ability to keep classes under control, which for most teachers meant keeping children at a distance. The image they presented to their pupils therefore was rather impersonal, almost one-dimensional.

By contrast, most younger children and many adolescents, particularly the less academic, wanted to see the teacher as a whole person. Some teachers, particularly when they were not yet secure in their professional role, were quite threatened by this more personal approach. They might also be new to life in a big city and suspect that their pupils were much more streetwise than they were. This might increase their tendency to stay in a narrowly professional didactic role which rather led to their seeing teaching as a one-way process, from teacher to taught. This did not suit lively youngsters who properly felt that learning is a two-way process and who wanted to be heard.

If teachers were to make the transition to using their whole personality, to relating much more fully to pupils, they needed support, particularly from senior staff. Many of them were afraid that if they allowed a more informal, more personal relationship, their class management would be threatened. And every teacher knew the nightmare of a class which was out of control.

Several teachers then individually discussed these issues. This is what they said:

> It's insecurity. Most teachers have a fear that what they are doing is open to criticism, so they say, 'Leave me on my pedestal where I feel in command'. Some staff are very afraid to give children any idea of themselves. Maybe they are like that in all aspects of their lives. But if you want to achieve change, slowly does it. People can't change radically overnight.

> I believe in being open with children, and I make it known that I am always available for them to talk to me privately if they want to. But there is a fear in some teachers that if you do this, children will take advantage of your relationship when in class and be more difficult to control. I think this is not so. Some teachers are afraid of letting the barriers down. They think it is unprofessional. But kids pick up this guardedness and resent it.

> Because I advise on careers, I am timetabled to see pupils individually. This gives me a good basis for working in the class group. While I agree wih pupil participation as it is practised in this school, it does not mean letting go of structure, control and leadership. The kids expect this. For some of our kids we are the only reliable thing in their lives. If you let things go too much, they think that you don't care about them. This is not what pupil participation is about.

> It is true that some teachers are quite afraid of letting children get close to them. I was myself at first, as a man teacher in an all-girls' school, and with many of them from very different cultural backgrounds. Also my subject is mathematics which does not obviously recommend itself to an emotional

approach. What changed me was that I was given a first year tutor group that I stayed with throughout their time in the school. That gives the kids a sense of security, and in fact it gave me one too. Do I think that all the time given to tutorial work is justified? It is if you are using the time properly. Some of it is directly relevant to academic work, preparing for exams, for example. And many of the children come from homes that are not able to help them much academically. But we also talk about other important issues, such as coping with boy friends. This is quite a problem for girls from much stricter cultural backgrounds. They have to learn to respect their parents' views but also to make their own decisions, maturely. If you want to help your pupils to self-discipline, you have to have developed a personal relationship with them. This our tutorial system allows.

Education is changing rapidly. Imparting knowledge is only a part of it. Learning in this school is a shared process. Why do other teachers resist these ideas? Perhaps we are afraid of criticism. But we shouldn't pretend to know it all. I tell children that I am still learning and that they have something to teach me. This school has a great tradition of caring for the total welfare of the children and they know it. If you are not prepared to give enough of yourself, you shouldn't go into teaching.

Drawing conclusions

It will be clear by now that the many teachers and pupils we talked to were not primarily interested in pupil participation for its own sake. If pressed they would all, no doubt, be prepared to say that they approved of it in principle. What they were interested in was running good schools. They wanted good opportunities for all pupils, those of high academic ability and those with learning difficulties, to develop their talents as fully as possible. They wanted all pupils, boys or girls, of whatever ethnic origin, of whatever social class, to feel valued. They also wanted effective schools with good examination results, good standards of behaviour and overall good morale. And from our brief observations they seemed to be achieving this.

Schools over the last few years have had to meet many challenges: not least the many changes brought about by the 1988 Education Act. Times of change can be threatening to morale. They can also provide opportunities for reappraisal. The schools we visited have not been afraid of change. They have used it positively, and to increase pupil participation, realising, as many of them said, that there is a resource which has traditionally remained largely untapped.

Three themes seem to need further exploration: the role of the headteacher and senior staff; the part that increased involvement might play in improving pupils' behaviour; and teachers' fears about giving a greater share of control to pupils.

The role of the headteacher and senior staff

It was crystal clear from our small sample that the capacity for leadership and the level of ability of the headteacher as well as of their ability to manage their staff were central to the success of the schools visited. This would be accepted as a self-evident truth in any educational discussion. To quote the Elton Report (DES, 1989b) on school morale: 'successful change can be achieved. The first and most important requirement is a positive commitment by the headteacher and other senior staff' (p.90).

In 1995, the Education Secretary, Gillian Shephard, announced plans to ensure that head teachers had better training and that their effectiveness is monitored more closely (Preston, 1995). This move reflected her conviction that head teachers are the most important influence on schools and that their role is critical in raising standards – a sentiment with which few would disagree.

Improving pupils' behaviour

With the 1993 Education Act and its Code of Practice, pupils' perceptions of the educational process and their emotional response to school is receiving ever wider attention. This statutory Code at last, after much consultation with professional groups, acknowledges that the pupil's perspective is important (Davie, 1994). The circular accompanying the Code, on *The Education of Children with Emotional and Behavioural Difficulties* (DfE, 1994c) states that it is policy that:

> the vast majority of chldren with emotional and behavioural difficulties will be educated in the mainstream classroom: the emotional development of children must continue to be a central concern for mainstream education. . . . there is a positive association between pupils' involvement and greater motivation and feelings of self-worth on their part (paras 16 and 31).

There is evidence, however, that whatever the official policy, exclusions from mainstream school are rising. A report by the Family Policy Studies Centre (Parsons, 1994) showed that exclusions from primary schools because of difficult behaviour had gone up from 3,000 in 1991–2 to between 7,000 and 8,000 in 1993–4. The Association of Metropolitan

Authorities (1995) noted an increase in exclusions which it considered to be due to the fact that head teachers had reduced their tolerance threshold for bad behaviour because of the pressures of the 1988 Act.

There is now an extensive literature on the perceptions pupils have of their school and of the need for teachers to understand this. Failures of communication lead to an escalation of problems:

> Emotional and behavioural difficulties are often embedded in the ways in which individuals perceive themselves and their environment: this refers to both the perspectives of the pupils themselves and the perceptions of them held by others. In these circumstances emotional and behavioural change stems from the articulation and analysis of these perceptions (Cooper, 1993).

Cronk (1987), after a long and careful study of teacher-pupil conflict in secondary schools, writes:

> If pupils know they could always criticise a teacher or the curriculum without being accused of rudeness: indeed, if they were taught ways of phrasing and presenting criticism which minimised the hurt to the person involved, while still making the point; if they were asked on a regular basis to evaluate lessons and suggest ways in which their teachers could improve their method; if teachers then took these criticisms seriously and in exchange gave reasons for their actions; and if all this were done on a regular basis, and solutions to differences of opinion were worked out together; then ....entrenched teacher-pupil conflict would never arise (p.209).

Teachers' fears

There is by now a considerable literature on what goes wrong for children emotionally in school. By contrast, work on the emotional experience of teaching is sparse. Yet anyone who has taught, particularly if in a badly-managed school, knows that teaching can be a nightmare. The demands of the job are complex and the most central task is learning to keep a class in order. Traditionally, this is something that young teachers have often been left to find out for themselves. Anyone who works with teachers knows that many have suffered severe shocks to their self-esteem, almost threats to their identity when faced with the reality of a difficult class. Woods (1990), writing about stress in teaching, describes a situation which many of us will recognise.

> Consider the following testimony from an English teacher who resigned at 28 after only three-and-a-half years teaching. At her last school, a comprehensive, 'a lot of the staff were scared and apprehensive. One woman teacher spent her lunch hours and breaks hiding in a lavatory. She was really

> frightened of the kids.' She herself had a totally uncooperative class,... a group of boys ...'were determined to give me a hard time...On one occasion I had hennaed my hair. I heard comments about this, and somebody asked in a loud stage whisper, whether I had enough left over to do my pubic hair. Then they called me a slag. I thought Christ, I don't need this'. ... Others suffered too: 'A lot of hardened teachers were quietly battling on. They talked about their problems – and the fact that nobody in authority seemed able to do anything to solve them. The teachers were left impotent. There was nothing they could do to make the children work.' ...She began to suffer from 'depression and stress' and to feel 'increasingly undervalued'. In the end 'the children forced her out'.

It would be a brave teacher who in a setting such as that would attempt greater consultation with their pupils. It is taken as a fact of life in work with children officially recognised as having emotional and behavioural difficulties that teachers who feel unsupported and unvalued will not be able to support and value their pupils, nor to manage them well, and this applies just as much to teachers in mainstream.

It is now widely accepted that there must be whole-school behaviour policies, explicit and owned by pupils, parents, staff and governors. The Circular on pupil behaviour and discipline, for example, accompanying the Code of Practice (DfE, 1994c) and based considerably on the Elton Report (DES, 1989b) emphasises this and says that, as part of school policy, teachers should: 'feel free to consult a senior member of staff without this being regarded as a failure....they should be able to feel confident that they have support and guidance available when they need it'.

Underlying all this must be a positive school ethos, which takes us back to the need for strong leadership. With this, teachers' self-esteem and confidence grow, and they may then be ready to exploit the potential that the teachers in this study identified. And, as one of the teachers interviewed put it, they might come fully to accept that, 'Teachers are very important in children's lives. Some of them seem to have difficulty in believing it'.

Part IV
The Voice of the Child with Special Educational Needs

CHAPTER 8

How Children with Emotional and Behavioural Difficulties View Professionals

Derrick Armstrong and David Galloway

Introduction

It is more than 25 years since the Plowden Report encouraged the notion of a child-centred curriculum in primary schools (CACE, 1967) and more than 15 years since the Warnock Report made special educational need a subject of every-day staffroom discussion (DES, 1978). Yet there is a conspicuous lack of evidence that concerns about the needs of children are a dominant feature in social and educational policy. Although increasing numbers of children are being identified as having 'special' needs of one sort or another, this trend has as much to do with 'league tables' and other responses to the National Curriculum as with child-centredness. Amongst these children are those seen as disadvantaged by social and environmental conditions, those who are believed to be ill-equipped physically or mentally to cope with the complexities of modern living, and those who by abuse or neglect have been psychologically damaged.

Running parallel to this increasing concern about children 'in need' has been a growth in the number of professional groups expressing a claim to expert knowledge in respect of children's needs. From psychologists to speech therapists, from educational social workers to teachers of English as a second language, the application of expert knowledge to the care and control of children has been a major phenomenon of the twentieth century. Countless books, as well as a considerable amount of research money, have been devoted to the expert opinions of professionals. Surprisingly little attention, however, has been paid to how the child makes sense of all this professional concern.

This chapter will attempt to remedy the imbalance by exploring children's perceptions of professional roles and by considering how these perceptions affect the way children behave. The chapter will draw on research evidence from an ESRC-funded project on 'Participant perspectives on the assessment of emotional and behavioural difficulties' to argue that assessment negotiations about children's needs take place within a framework over which children have little or no control. As a consequence, children may not only be denied a genuine voice; their participation may also contribute to an internalisation of negative self-identities.

The problems with this 'child-deficit' model of assessment are well known (Galloway *et al.*, 1994) but the difficulties in replacing it with something more positive are formidable. The 1993 Educational Act requires professionals to identify the child's special educational needs. More seriously, a critical evaluation of the quality of teaching and resources in the child's class is seldom an explicit part of the assessment process. Yet to assume that these are irrelevant to a child's learning and/or behaviour is at best naive. Children may be more aware of this than their professional 'partners' which can be one reason why they *have so little to say*. Advocating children's involvement in decision-making, divorced from an analysis of the decision-making process, and in particular the constraints under which professionals operate, may make us feel better but does not necessarily improve matters for the child.

Background

It is only in comparatively recent times that recognition has started to be given to the unique perspective of the child as an authentic interpretation of the child's reality. It is, therefore, important to gain access to that perspective and to acknowledge its importance as a factor contributing to decisions being taken about children. Historically, children have not only been disenfranchised in the decision-making processes that directly affect them but they have frequently been seen as little more than the property of their parents (see Chapter 2). Even now, despite some increased public awareness of how children are made vulnerable by being denied a voice in decisions affecting their lives, the evidence of involvement remains patchy and the evidence of professional uncertainty about how to enhance the child's role is plentiful. The Cleveland child abuse case highlighted the pitfalls faced by professionals in their attempts to act in the interests of children; it also emphasised the consequences of ignoring child testimonies. Significantly, the report of the inquiry into this case recommended that professionals should always listen carefully to children and take what they say seriously, maintaining that 'the views and wishes of the child, particularly as to what should happen to him/her, should be taken into account by the professionals involved with their problems' (Butler-Sloss, 1988, p.245).

In view of these developments it is perhaps surprising to find that with regard to educational decision-making children remain very much the 'property' of their parents. Indeed, Rosenbaum and Newell (1991) have argued that it is in respect of the child's role in *educational* decision-making that the United Nations Convention on the Rights of Children is most seriously disregarded in Britain today. Policy towards children with special educational needs to some extent stands out as a exception to this, although it is clear that the principles of consulting children whose special needs are being assessed and of involving them in decision-making have been tacked on very much as an afterthought.

The inclusion in the Code of Practice on the Identification and Assessment of SEN of a clear statement upholding the principle and value of listening to the child's views has been widely applauded. As we will argue, though, these general statements are not unproblematic and indeed may considerably over-simplify the difficulties encountered by professionals in gaining access to children's perspectives and involving them in the decision-making process. Moreover, they may over-simplify the implications for the child of participation in an assessment.

The general principle of involving children in decision-making raises three questions:

1. How is the involvement of children to be achieved in practice?
2. What is the child's perception of the assessment process and how does this influence strategies adopted by the child during the assessment?
3. What outcomes, unintentional as well as intentional, are being served by the child's involvement?

Aims and scope of the research

Between 1989 and 1991 we carried out research in three LEAs covering five geographical areas, looking at the formal assessment of 29 children aged between 5 and 16 who had been identified, usually by their teachers, as having emotional and behavioural difficulties (Galloway *et al.*, 1994). With the cooperation of clients and professionals, one of us (DA) observed the main parts of each child's assessment, including psychologists' interviews with children and parents, medical examinations and other interviews and meetings (e.g., case conferences). Subsequently interviews were held with each participant. One of the areas we were particularly interested in investigating was that of children's perceptions of the assessment and decision-making process and how these could affect children's behaviour during the assessment. In addition, retrospective interviews about their assessments were conducted with 18 children who had been placed within the previous 12 months either in a residential school or special unit for children with emotional and behavioural difficulties.

Working with children. the professional interview

Gaining access to children's perspectives requires skill in communicating meanings to children and understanding the meanings embedded in children's language and behaviour. Where meanings are imposed on children's accounts by adults, these are likely to result in distortion of the meanings used by children. Adult perceptions of children's beliefs and perspectives may be inadequate or inaccurate unless grounded in the meanings used by children. Yet this poses two interrelated and crucial problems for professionals. First, being willing to listen to what children have to say is far from straightforward. Avoiding the pitfalls that can arise when the child's views are mediated through an adult's professional view of the world involves considerable skill and empathetic understanding. Yet the demands placed on teachers, psychologists and other professionals to 'process' large numbers of children through the 1993 Act procedures makes Gersch's (1987) description of the conventional role allotted to the child in the assessment process understandable:

> Although the process and purpose of assessment may vary from professional to professional, and indeed there are different emphases on tests, observation and other techniques, children themselves are conventionally ascribed a subservient role in the whole assessment process. They are often expected to carry out specified tasks, answer specific questions, undertake written activities or follow set procedures. The child is generally seen as a relatively 'passive object', and assessment is viewed as something which is 'done to the child' rather than involving the child very actively (p.154).

Our own research very much confirmed this picture. For instance, despite their awareness of the DES/DfE advice and support for it in principle, there was little evidence of educational psychologists adopting systematic procedures for gaining access to the child's point of view and involving them in decision-making. Interviews with all but three children in our sample focused upon psychometric measures of 'intelligence' and reading attainment. Our observations of assessment interviews with children did suggest that these psychologists attempted to explain something about the assessment procedures, yet they appeared to find difficulty in pitching their explanations at a level that made sense to the children.

Second, the assumptions made by professionals when interpreting children's accounts may lead to the rationality of those accounts being questioned and consequently to children's wishes and views being disregarded 'in their own interests'. In such cases the pragmatic decision to disregard the child's views often conceals an epistemological problem: how can adults know that they *have* gained a valid understanding of what a child *really* meant. Children's disempowerment can be brought about by adults' assumptions about what is best for them. These assumptions can all too easily be compounded by inappropriate methods of listening. This was illustrated during the assessment of one of the children in our study, Peter. Peter's silence and lack of cooperation when questioned by a psychologist about his own wishes was interpreted as supporting evidence obtained from personality testing which suggested Peter might be 'suffering from a personality disorder'. However, when interviewed by a researcher, who was seen by Peter not to have a role in the assessment, Peter confided that he was frightened about being taken away from his family and that it was 'The psychologist [who] wants to send me away'. For Peter, his anxiety about the role of the psychologist led him to distrust the psychologist's intentions and hence to his refusal to cooperate in the assessment. Thus, whilst the psychologist interpreted Peter's behaviour at interview as the outcome of a 'personality disorder', Peter's own account of his behaviour during the interview was given in terms of his expectations of the assessment process itself.

Children's perceptions of the assessment process, its purpose and outcomes

Despite DES/DfE advice about partnership with children, our interviews with children indicated that they rarely believed genuine attempts had been made to involve them in the assessment process, or even to encourage them to contribute. Many of these children appeared to be unaware how decisions had been reached. Nearly all of the children in our sample did remember being seen by a psychologist yet few were able to give any account of what the psychologist's role in the assessment had been when they were subsequently interviewed. For one child, however, the visit by the psychologist had been 'to help him [the psychologist] find out *what was wrong with me*'.

For this child at least the interview with the psychologist had reinforced his perception of himself being the 'problem'. The account given by another child in this sample again illustrates how a child's perception of the role of professionals identifies himself as the 'problem', yet this account in addition illustrates the confusion many children had about the roles of professionals they had seen:

> I had a brain scan. This thing on my head with lots of wires to see if there was owt wrong with me, if I was dyslexic or what. I don't know what they said about it.

This lack of information left children at a serious disadvantage when trying to understand the situation they were in and how to respond to it. After Susan was told to attend a medical examination as part of her assessment, she reported feeling 'nervous' and 'dreading going', but she didn't know why she felt this way other than a fear of the unknown. After the medical, Susan felt none the wiser: 'I don't think she found anything wrong with me but she never told me'.

In another case, the assessment procedures were seen by Tony as providing him with no opportunity to articulate what, for him, were very complex, and to some extent contradictory, views about his position now and what he wanted to happen in the future. Taken at face value he appeared to have nothing to contribute: 'I didn't say owt because I didn't have owt to say', but once the exterior of 'helplessness' was probed it was possible to see how, in part at least, it had originated in Tony's perception of the power professionals had exercised over him in the past. Talking to a researcher about the background to his recent placement in a residential special school, Tony described how he had been moved first from a mainstream school to a day special school, then back into a different mainstream school on a trial basis. Following the success of this 'trial', Tony was returned full-time to a third mainstream school before being placed in a residential school after his mainstream reintegration broke down:

> I left it [the day special school] because the teachers wanted to try me in a normal school. I went to a [mainstream] school one afternoon a week and was getting on well. I then went full-time to a different [mainstream school] and didn't get on at all ... .I used to take a nice walk, which was 25 miles, round to

> the special school to see the kids and the teachers. I wish I'd never left there. I would have gone back if I'd had the chance. I would have told them if they'd asked, but I wouldn't tell them if they didn't because I wanted to be in a normal school.

Children's involvement: who gains?

Advocates of children's involvement in assessment frequently appear to assume either that assessment is in the child's interests or that, if it is not, the child's contribution will help professionals to understand why it is not. The former assumption is at least questionable, its validity depending not only upon a detailed understanding of the motivations and actions of the different parties involved in an assessment but also upon an analysis of the tensions and conflicts leading to the decision to carry out an assessment. The latter assumption similarly depends upon a belief in professional benevolence which may not be justified, but also ignores inequalities in the power of different participants to pursue their own interests in the outcome of the assessment.

With regard to the practical dimension of children's involvement, the cooperation of the latter may on occasions enable teachers and other professionals to work more effectively, but this falls short of a partnership based on mutual respect, recognition of complementary areas of expertise or knowledge and a willingness to learn from each other. The cornerstone of the 1981 and 1993 Acts is the identification and assessment of children who have (unmet) needs. This conceptualises children's difficulties in terms of 'needs', which imply a deficit in those areas, whilst conceptualising the 'needs' of significant adults (be they teachers or parents) in terms of the power the latter have to define the problem (as they do when a child is referred for formal assessment). By identifying children as being 'in need', they and their parents can be denied the opportunity and power to define aspects of the social context as relevant to the way in which needs have been produced and represented. By contrast, the power of professionals and, to a lesser extent, parents, to determine consensual meanings applying within a particular context, by invoking official procedures which then serve to legitimate those meanings, enables them to represent their own needs in terms of the child's difficulties.

From the perspective of many of the children in our research, the decision to initiate an assessment was interpreted as itself implying the subordination of their account to that of the adults who had requested the assessment. Even though children might acknowledge that they had some responsibility for the problems they were now encountering, where an assessment was seen as being a response to teachers' or parents' perceptions of the 'problem', children almost invariably saw the assessment as part of their punishment. Nineteen of the children explicitly referred to the assessment in these terms.

Darren, for example, believed his assessment had been started because his teachers were 'saying I was the worst first year'. In a research interview, Darren contrasted his teachers' views about his aggressive behaviour with his own account of the problems he faced in secondary school:

> There were a lot of people aggravating me because I wasn't bright. I was more or less the thickest in the class and I used to smash out at them .... I got on with the teachers bad. They just didn't know what my problems were .... I used to always get taken the rip out of and that was the trouble really. I never bothered to listen. I just sat there making jokes.

Darren's psychologist did make some effort to question him about how he saw things at school but Darren was not very forthcoming. Later, in talking to the researcher, Darren maintained that:

> There was nothing I could say really because they wouldn't have me back in school .... I didn't want to be away from my family and friends but he [the psychologist] put me here [residential school]. He's the one who got me sent away.

Far from providing him with an opportunity to put forward his point of view for genuine consideration, Darren saw his referral to the psychologist as an expression of the power the school had over him. For Darren, his powerlessness did not lie in any intentional or neglectful failure on the part of the psychologist to provide him with an opportunity to say what he wanted. Rather the roots of Darren's powerlessness lay in his inability to control the framework of assumptions upon which the decision to initiate an assessment had been predicated. Thus from the outset the psychologist was cast by Darren, along with every other professional involved in his assessment, as *a priori* an enemy.

Thus, negotiations about the child's needs took place within a framework over which the child had little control, i.e. the referral procedures under the 1981 Act (and the 1993 Act has done nothing to change this). This is an important consideration when evaluating the implications of 'the child's right to be heard'. Listening to children is not something that takes place in a vacuum. One might wish to assume that professional decision-making is guided by nothing more than humanitarian benevolence and that in consequence a deeper understanding of the child's viewpoint will allow the professional to exercise a more rational judgement. On the other hand, it is worth noting that in the Code of Practice (DfE, 1994a) the principle of the child's right to be heard is couched in terms of the child being 'encouraged to participate in decision-making about provision to meet their special educational needs'. In other words, the professionals' assumption that the child has special educational needs is taken by the Code as valid. In theory this encourages children to contribute to discussion about how and where their special needs should be met. The logical problem here is that the discussion is predicated on a consensus about the nature of those special needs. Children can only contribute to debate about meeting their special needs if they have first contributed to the assessment of these needs. When the problem lies at least partly with the school, for example poor teaching or inadequate curriculum resources, it is very difficult for children to make a contribution that is likely to be taken seriously. However diplomatic the language, a claim that, 'I am failing to make progress, and behaving badly, because I have been badly taught', is not likely to be well received. Moreover, educational psychologists who endorse such a view may find that their relationship with the school's head and class teachers has seriously deteriorated.

In these circumstances the child's participation is almost inevitably based on the professionals' prior assumptions. The child's participation may influence decisions about whether or not her/his needs match the criteria used by other participants, but by participation the child implicitly, if unintentionally, reinforces the legitimacy of the framework.

Constraints on professionals

There are many reasons why children behave in the ways that they do and teachers, psychologists and other professionals working with children are rarely unsympathetic to the difficult circumstances in the home, the school and elsewhere which many children experience as a normal (and sometimes abnormal) part of growing up. Professional judgements and actions in these situations are often characterised (as they are in the Warnock Report [DES, 1978] and latterly in the Code of Practice on the Identification and Assessment of Special Educational Needs [DfE, 1994a]) as driven by a disinterested concern with the truth and an interest in the best possible outcome for the client who, it is usually assumed, is the child. This may well be an accurate representation of how professionals would like to see themselves but it is also a simplistic and one-sided view.

There are many pressures encountered by professionals working in education, from a variety of sources, and in the context of these pressures professionals may feel constrained to define problems in terms of difficulties children present to others. In other words, professionals may not be in a position simply to assess a child's needs because those needs must be understood in the context of the different expectations other clients may reasonably have of professional advice, support and action. For instance, teachers have professional responsibilities towards children in their classes (and towards the parents of those children) who are affected by the disruptive behaviour of other children. Similarly, educational psychologists must also have regard to the legitimate expectations schools and LEAs have of receiving a professional service. Referrals for assessment do not arise solely from a disinterested concern to establish if a child has special educational needs. The expectations teachers, parents and others have of the assessment at the outset are likely to exert a crucial influence over its final outcome. The expectations often include the acquisition of additional resources, the removal of the child from school, or a promise to act quickly if matters deteriorate in the future.

Johnson (1972), in an analysis of the relationship between professionals and the state in modern society, has argued that the state comes between professionals and their clients to define clients' needs and to specify the parameters within which those needs are to be met. Through this mediation professionals are incorporated into the decision-making machinery of government and are made dependent on the state. How this may operate within the procedures for assessing special educational needs is evident from the pressures experienced by psychologists in our study who were well aware of LEA expectations that they should not make recommendations without considering the realities of available provision. In accepting these 'realities' and attempting to identify the needs of their child clients within the context of the resources likely to be made available by their LEA, psychologists frequently found themselves having to balance the different interests of different 'clients'. Each of these clients – child, parents, teachers and LEA – might have legitimate expectations of the psychologist but each might also have potentially conflicting needs. The consequent ethical and professional dilemmas could seriously affect the ability of the psychologist to represent the interests of any of their clients (see Armstrong and Galloway, 1992).

Conclusion

There is clearly a growing concern amongst professionals who are involved in the assessment of children with special educational needs that these children should have the right to be heard in relation to decisions that affect their futures. This concern has in part arisen out of formal recognition of children's rights, particularly as embodied in the 1989 Children Act and more recently in the 1994 Code of Practice. It is also a reflection of professional experience in this area which, building on the parent-professional partnerships emphasised in the Warnock Report, is beginning to recognise how listening to children can enhance the effectiveness of professional interventions. Yet, in practice, there is still a long way to go. The requirements of the 1994 Code of Practice do not provide any specific guidance as to how children's views should be ascertained and in consequence 'good practice' continues to be a matter for individual professional judgement.

There is a need for specialised training to assist professionals to enhance their skills in this area. The pioneering work of Gersch (1987; 1990) in the use of child self-report procedures in assessments does suggest how training in this area may be developed. This work has built on the strengths of records of achievement and pupil profiling (Broadfoot, 1986). However, as we have argued in this chapter, the difficulties professionals experience in gaining access to the child's perspective are not simply a reflection of a lack of skills and training in these areas. A more deep-rooted problem stems from the assessment system itself.

Formal assessment under the 1981 Act was frequently reactive and the 1993 Act and the Code of Practice does not remove that tendency. It is often initiated by teachers in response to situations in which they no longer feel themselves to have the professional skills to manage learning and/or control behaviour effectively (Armstrong *et al.*, 1993). Whether the stages of assessment envisaged in the Code of Practice will change this remains to be seen. The involvement of outside professionals at this stage may also in consequence be primarily reactive to the situation as defined by teachers. This can create professional dilemmas for those professionals which then affect their work with pupils and schools (Armstrong and Galloway, 1992). The ambiguity of the psychologist's role, in particular, may seriously undermine their ability to gain access to children's thinking and to represent the interests of children. In part, disregard for the child's perspective follows from the demands of a complex situation in which the needs of competing clients (school, parents, LEA and child) determine the extent to which the child's perspective is *allowed to be relevant*. However, just as importantly, the child's understanding of the assessment process and in particular of the role of different professionals in that process is also likely to have a significant effect on the child's understanding of the consequences of participation and therefore upon his/her willingness to participate or upon the strategies adopted by the child during the assessment.

Exhorting professionals to take account of the child's perspective, although appearing perfectly laudable when stated abstractly as a matter of principle, may actually have the unintended consequence of further disempowering the child in those procedures. In the absence of any critique of the fundamental assumptions that underlie the decision to carry out an assessment, a child's participation may implicitly serve to legitimise those assumptions. For some children, non-participation is the only means by which they feel able to express their opposition to the ways in which their needs have been conceptualised by professionals. Whilst participation may be seen as implying an acceptance of that basic framework, active opposition is likely to be taken as confirmation of the difficulties and/or deficits which beset that child. The difficulties professionals experience in gaining access to children's thinking is a direct consequence of the very perceptive realisation by many children of what for professionals, motivated by a belief in children's rights and in their own professional responsibilities towards children as clients, is a very unpalatable truth.

It does not follow from this that any assessment of a child's needs will be implicitly based upon a child-deficit model and therefore will inevitably lead to a rejection of the child's perspective. What does follow, however, is that for children to be genuinely empowered in assessments of educational need, the aim of assessment must be to identify how the experience of learning itself needs to be changed to give children their right to an education. This involves far more than increasing the awareness and updating the skills of professionals; it requires a radical reconceptualisation and restructuring of professional practice in terms of the civil rights of the children with whom they are in partnership.

Acknowledgements

This chapter is based on research carried out with Research Grant No. R 000 23 1393 from the ESRC, and the Research Council's support is gratefully acknowledged.

CHAPTER 9

Listening to Children with Special Educational Needs

Philippa Russell

Introduction

The implementation of the Children Act 1989 and the UK ratification of the UN Convention on the Rights of the Child have raised the profile of children's involvement in decision-making and also underlined the responsibilities of parents and professionals to take account of children's views and to facilitate those views being heard. The Introduction to the *Code of Practice on the Identification and Assessment of Special Educational Needs* (DfE, 1994a) states (for the first time in education guidance) that:

> Special educational provision will be most effective when those responsible take into account the ascertainable wishes of the child concerned, considered in the light of his or her age and understanding.

The Code of Practice, like Part III of the 1993 Education Act and the 1981 Act which preceded it, reinforces the importance of parents as having a 'crucial bearing upon the child's educational progress and the effectiveness of any school-based action.' But it breaks new ground in also acknowledging the practical benefits of similar partnerships with children (i.e., the recognition that children often have important and relevant information and their support will be crucial to the effective implementation of any individual education programme) and secondly, that education services must acknowledge the principle that children have a right to be heard. Therefore they should be encouraged to participate in decision-making about provision to meet their special needs.

The Code of Practice recognises that positive pupil involvement is unlikely to occur spontaneously. Careful attention, guidance and encouragement will be required to help pupils respond relevantly and fully. Many young people with special needs may be unaware of the significance of their disability or difficulty and currently few are given direct responsibility for their own progress. But the new school-based and statutory assessment arrangements will require some radical rethinking about what pupils think and feel. Schools will, for example, find themselves discussing the purpose of a particular assessment arrangement (children have rights under the Children Act 1989 – see below – to refuse examination or treatment if they are judged sufficiently mature to make such a decision). Many children with special educational needs have little self-confidence and low self-esteem. The effective use of pupils' reports, records of achievement and systematic feedback to the child concerned will be critical in engaging their interest and in demonstrating their real possibility of progression. Section 2.37 of the Code encourages schools to consider how they:

- involve pupils in decision-making processes;
- determine the pupil's level of participation, taking into account approaches to assessment and intervention which are suitable for his or her age, ability and past experiences;
- record pupils' views in identifying their difficulties, setting goals, agreeing a development strategy, monitoring and reviewing progress;
- involve pupils in implementing individual education plans.

Although the Children Act 1989 established the over-arching principle of partnership with children (and many local authorities have made good progress in working directly with children in assessment), the most detailed guidance so far has been given on children looked after by the local authority, i.e., children who are living away from home and for whom the local authority must in consequence prepare and review regularly a child care plan. The Code of Practice, however, sets out general principles for direct pupil involvement throughout both the school-based stages of assessment and in statutory assessment and review.

In considering partnership with children, it is important to acknowledge that many parents will be reluctant to discuss their child's disability or special need. There is ample documentation of the process of adaptation to a diagnosis of disability and the struggles encountered by many families in arriving at a positive picture of their child and becoming confident about the best way forward. In some instances a medical condition or disability will have long-term implications for parents *and* children (for example with muscular dystrophy or in an AIDS/HIV-related illness) where the child will have to adapt to a very different future and where there may be a real prospect of deterioration or even death in the adolescent years.

The effective involvement of children at the first school-based stages of assessment, (in particular in systematically recording their personal perceptions of any difficulties and how they might be addressed), will be critical for the proposed new arrangements for statutory assessment. Section 3.8 of the Code of Practice reminds schools that when they refer children to the LEA for statutory assessment, they should submit information on 'the recorded views of parents and, where appropriate, children on the earlier stages of assessment and any action and support to date'. The new requirement to provide written individual education plans at stages two and three of school-based assessment should provide a framework for such recording and for positive action. But assessment can be very threatening for parents. It may appear even more threatening for a pupil, particularly where he or she fears exclusion from a school or is experiencing a loss of self-esteem because of poor performance as compared to friends. Statutory assessment may similarly pose problems, particularly if the pupil concerned is uncertain as to how he or she may express views or how those views will be considered if they are perhaps critical of a particular aspect of school life or of family or other professionals within the child's local community.

Involving pupils in assessment of special educational needs

As noted above, the involvement of pupils with special educational needs in assessment, intervention and review will be a process for all concerned. Over the past few years, there have been important initiatives in working directly with pupils. Irvine Gersch' work in Waltham Forest in developing student reports has important lessons for the whole education field (and for social services departments which are currently working to develop similar models for the direct involvement of children 'in need' and with disabilities in their own assessments). Gersch (1994) acknowledges that some young people will need support, but emphasises that:

> the aim of the exercise is to encourage the young person's active involvement in the assessment process. The adult helper will need to know the young person well, to remain impartial and yet to know when to prompt and encourage without implanting their own ideas.

A challenge for all children's services is how children with special needs may indeed be known well and their views recorded in an assessment process. Gersch (1987) has identified a number of key issues in effective assessment. To begin with, the assessor needs to 'get inside children's shoes'. Gersch graphically describes the experience of an HMI who tracked children round a school for a week: his perspective of what it was really like to be living in the child's world changed. He notes that most children with special needs are subject to multiple assessments, for many of which they will be questioned, examined and may be completely confused about the outcome of the exercise.

Gersch also identifies three key issues which have to be addressed in such assessments. First, there are *pragmatic* advantages in listening to children. Like parents, they hold a wide range of information; like parents, they understand the factors external to school which may be contributing to a particular problem. Second, there are *moral* issues at stake. Equal opportunities policies have in general treated disability issues as the Cinderella of the service. And third, there are *legal* duties to listen to children, both within the new framework for the assessment of special educational needs set out within the Code of Practice and within the Children Act 1989.

However, the direct involvement of pupils will be challenging to schools, many of whom have not yet fully involved parents in the assessment and involvement of pupils with special educational needs. The implementation of the Children Act has shown that parents do not necessarily agree amongst themselves and they certainly do not always agree with their children. Most importantly, children themselves see very clearly when they have problems. A self-advocacy group of young people with moderate learning difficulties (*The Friday Book*, National Children's Bureau, 1990) highlighted some of the practical problems which pupils may face on a day-to-day basis and about which neither their school nor parents may be aware. Jackie, in *The Friday Book*, notes that:

> We all went to special schools for slow learners. We'd have preferred to have gone to ordinary schools. I didn't want to go to a special school. It was my Mum's choice...she said don't argue!

Jackie goes on to comment that her teachers stood up for her when local children called her 'spastic' and 'handicapped'. When she moved to an ordinary school, she felt the stigma of having the extra help she needed:

> Even though my reading and writing were good, they still gave me extra lessons at school. They didn't give extra lessons to people who couldn't read

> and write... but if you wanted home-work, you had to ask for it. I used to ask for it and they used to say 'you can't have it because you're not bright enough to have homework'. I was behind in maths – but they wouldn't take me by the hand and take me to the classroom and keep me behind an hour and help me to do it.

Jackie goes on to comment that:

> I think it is right what my headmaster said about getting teased in an ordinary school ... but when you leave school and meet a gang of boys, they tease you for going to a special school. Even now when I have left school, people round where I live give me funny looks in the street, because they know I went to a special school.

Jackie's acute observations of her own situation, her desire to be 'ordinary' and her wish for help in achieving literacy and numeracy could have been usefully incorporated within an individual education plan. Aware of her learning difficulties, acutely conscious of the stigma which 'special school' conveyed within her local community, and resentful of what she saw as her mother's 'bossiness' in decision-making, she looked back at her educational experiences with some bitterness. But Jackie's feelings are none the less positive. She was persuaded to share them with other young people with special educational needs and with a teacher and her parents through a self-advocacy group. Jackie would have welcomed a programme of support in school; she was clear about her priorities in terms of getting future employment – namely basic literacy and numeracy. Her poor self-esteem would have been helped by a recognition by her teachers that she was trying hard and that the transition from special to mainstream school had been very stressful. The bullying and name-calling could have been dealt with if there had been a clear school behaviour policy and if Jackie had felt able to discuss her fears with a teacher. Most importantly, Jackie's mother could have been involved and given greater expectations for the daughter she frankly saw as 'sweet but backward' and whom she did not know how to help.

Jackie's views about her life are also an important reminder of certain key assessments within the new 1993 Act arrangements where the views of pupils will be critical. The Transition Plan replaces the former 13-plus statutory reassessment. From the first annual review after a young person's fourteenth birthday, an annual Transition Plan pulls together the views of the school, any relevant education professionals within the LEA, social services and health, the careers service and parents and the young person him or herself. The Code of Practice acknowledges that participation will not always be easy and suggests that the 'named person' might perform a support role. Section 6.46 of the Code of Practice sets out a range of key questions for young people, including:

- What information do young people need in order to be able to make informed choices?
- What local arrangements exist for advocacy, befriending or representation if required?
- How *can* young people be encouraged to contribute to their own Transition Plan and planning for the future?
- If young people are attending a residential school or living away from home, are there special issues relating to the location of post-school services to be addressed?
- What are the young person's own wishes and aspirations for the future and how can these be met?

The success or otherwise of the Transition Plan will only be achieved if there is earlier involvement of pupils in assessment – with realistic understandings of the nature of their difficulties and how they might be resolved. The Transition Plan in particular will necessitate some potentially sensitive and negative discussion of the full implication of a disability and special need in adult life. It will also highlight any difficulties within the family and differences of opinion about the future. But it is also a new opportunity for an honest and open discussion between pupil, parents, school and all concerned about constructive approaches for the future and some new partnerships based on mutual respect, the setting of clear goals and a regular review process to which the pupil must contribute.

Listening to children with special educational needs: lessons from the Children Act 1989

The Children Act 1989 places new duties on social services departments to involve children in planning their own futures, *including* children with disabilities and special educational needs. But, as Volume 6 (Children with Disabilities) of the DH's guidance and regulations on the Children Act 1989 notes:

> There is a fine balance between giving the child (with a disability or special educational needs) a voice and encouraging them to make informed decisions – and over-burdening them with decision-making procedures where they have insufficient experience and knowledge to make appropriate judgements without additional support. Learning to make well informed choices and to

> make some mistakes should be part of every child's experience. Children and young people should be given the chance to exercise choice and their views should be taken seriously .... plans should be explained, discussed and if necessary reassessed in the light of the child's views (DH, 1992).

The same guidance goes on to note that children with disabilities and special needs, whilst having 'the same rights to access to information as others', may have great difficulty in accessing these rights if they have communication or mobility difficulties or if their ability to show sufficient understanding is not acknowledged. Importantly, Volume 6 of the Children Act guidance reminds us that,

> their [children with disabilities or special educational needs] ability to give consent or refusal to any action, including assessment, examination or treatment is only limited by the general conditions relating to sufficient understanding which apply to other children under the Children Act (DH, 1992).

Participation in decision-making, whether in an education or social work context, may often be threatening for children and their parents and related professionals. Participation will be a token exercise, unless there is clear understanding about the *consequences* of decisions, as well as about the rationale for making them. Many children with special needs have low self-esteem and few positive expectations for their own future. Assessment will be potentially further damaging, if it merely records what children *cannot* do and underlines differences from the all-important peer group. The use of positive recording (for example Records of Achievement) and the recognition of even small successes will be crucial in enabling children to feel sufficient empowerment to be able to contribute to discussions about the best way forward.

Teachers and schools may usefully look to some of the preliminary work on the involvement of children with disabilities within social services departments, in the context of Children Act implementation. The first national inspection of services for children with disabilities under the Children Act 1989 (SSI, 1994) set standards for future inspections and for local authorities wishing to establish policies for work with disabled children. The same report recognised the importance of education in contributing information on individual children's lives and reminded local authorities that Schedule 2, Paragraph 3 of the Children Act states that they may make assessments of a child's needs at the same time as other assessments, such as assessment under the 1981 Act, commenting that:

> Assessments under the 1981 Education Act were a central focus for parents and appeared to be the major forum outside of multi-disciplinary child development assessment centres where inter-agency work was developing.

The report was critical of many social services departments' approaches to assessment of children with disabilities, which often seemed so informal that 'some parents were unaware that an assessment had taken place', but underlined the importance of creating *new* partnerships with LEAs, where there was likely to be a considerable body of knowledge about individual children. The Report made a number of specific recommendations about how partnerships with children and young people in assessment might be developed and the recommendations in question have equal relevance to education services, namely:

The importance of recognising that different parts of a service will be at different stages in working directly with children. Currently there is much more evidence of working with parents, but some staff will be very reluctant to work with children because of concerns about the implications of discussing complex and sometimes potentially negative information.

Consulting with children with disabilities or special educational needs requires expertise and staff may need additional training.

Consultation with pupils must also take into account awareness of any linguistic, cultural, religious or social needs.

Access to independent advocacy, representation or befriending schemes may be crucial for some children (particularly for those 'looked after' by the local authority).

Some children with disabilities or special needs have additional communication problems and accurate interpretation of their views and their representation in decision-making may be problematic – particularly when there is a disagreement with the parents about the service being offered.

Participation skills can be learned and children who are *routinely* involved in decision-making when things go well will have fewer difficulties when a disagreement occurs.

Access to complaints procedures are important (the SSI report preceded the introduction of complaints procedures into schools' SEN policies and the issuing of guidance on the SEN tribunals).

The SSI Report concluded that there was a genuine commitment to listening to children with special needs amongst all the social services departments concerned, but that:

> There was wide disparity in the level and skills of those working with disabled children ... this demonstrated the importance of a comprehensive training and staff development programme amongst both the generic workforce carrying out a range of child-care duties *and* for disability workers who carry responsibility for children.

The lesson for education services from this study of current social services practice and policy is that mainstream and specialist staff need common training and that listening to children with special needs requires whole-services approaches. To achieve this goal, the SSI recommend:

Clear policies and guidance within the service for all staff on ascertaining the wishes and feelings of children.

Written procedures for everyone (including parents) to ensure that children's wishes and feelings must be observed.

Training in disability awareness/special needs for all concerned.

Working with children in a secure situation at a pace and in a manner which takes account of the child's special needs or disability, age and understanding.

Always recording the views of children; this record should be confirmed as accurate with the child and shared with the parents.

Assistance is provided during any discussions to enable children with specific communication needs to express themselves fully.

Any linguistic, ethnic or other needs are taken into account.

The extent to which children's wishes and feelings are taken into account is carefully monitored, including in discussion with parents and carers.

If serious differences of opinion occur, the agency should endeavour to find an independent advocate or representative for the child (this could be another neutral professional or a member of an advocacy scheme, if one exists). SSI notes that *parents* may act as advocates for their children.

The SSI recommendations provide useful guidance for implementing the spirit of pupil involvement in the Code of Practice and within schools' SEN policies. They also provide a salutary reminder that the involvement of children with disabilities or special needs will be *everybody's* business and that schools and professionals in education services may usefully work together with colleagues in health and social services to develop common procedures.

Special educational needs with a child who is 'looked after' by the local authority

The Children Act 1989 introduced the new concept of accommodation (whether in foster or residential placements) as a service for children 'in need' without the former stigma of being 'in care' and with a strong focus upon 'looking after' children rather than 'removing' them from homes and local communities. Although some children will continue to be accommodated by a local authority under statutory procedures related to child protection matters, the vast majority of children will be considered as having a form of 'shared care' within which parents will continue to play a significant role. The Children Act recognises the importance of multi-disciplinary planning for such children, and even children living away from home for short periods of time (respite care) will be expected to have a child-care plan, which involves parents and children, which is regularly reviewed and which *must* state the arrangements for a child's education whilst looked after by the local authority.

As the Audit Commission (1994), in its report *Seen But Not Heard*, noted, 'Social services departments and education need to accept joint ownership of the problem of disrupted education of children "looked after" by the local authority and work together to find solutions'. The numbers of children "looked after" by local authorities who have special educational needs is unquantified, but the introduction of the school-based stages of assessment within the Code of Practice is likely to increase the numbers of pupils who are 'looked after' and in school who become involved in school-based assessment. Schools will therefore need to create new working relationships not only with social services but with all those – such as foster parents or care staff – who are exercising parental responsibility for a child at any one time. Many schools are probably unaware of the size of the population of children within the 'looked after' category. The Audit Commission (1994) has estimated that in 1993, 52,100 children were being 'looked after' by the local authority. In that same year, 38,000 children ceased to be 'looked after', with another 32,500 children starting to be looked after.

The DfE's circulars on *Pupils with Problems* (1994c) identify some of the challenges. Circular 13/94, *Children Looked After by the Local Authority*, reminds schools of the complex, often disruptive and sometimes damaging causes of a child being 'looked after' by a local authority. It also reminds us that many pupils will regard this as a dubious status, which they may be reluctant to disclose or discuss for fear of teasing or hostility from fellow pupils. The Circular comments that:

> Robust support systems for individual children are needed, and sensitive, fair and consistent management by school staff .... head teachers in primary schools and year tutors in secondary schools are in a position to hold a watching brief for all children being looked after in their school or year respectively, to provide advice and guidance in relation to individual children and, where necessary, to coordinate the pastoral needs of the children concerned.

Some schools will find the 'giving of advice and guidance' very challenging, particularly where the pupil concerned is causing problems because of difficult behaviour and where there is uncertainty about both the origins and the management of that behaviour in a school context. However, there are some practical models of support and intervention which can be developed to meet local need. The SSI Inspection of Services for children with disabilities (op. cit.) noted that in some authorities, the use of individual representatives or advocates was helpful when a child or young person needed to be involved in sensitive discussion and decision-making. The Audit Commission (1994) visited one authority where education and social services had jointly appointed an education liaison officer whose role was to work directly with individual schools in helping them to create cooperative approaches to working directly with pupils with problems or special educational needs and to tackle difficulties effectively. The education liaison officer supported 34 children during 1991/2, of whom only two were permanently excluded from school following her intervention. Her approach included offering support and encouragement of a practical nature, such as creating the right environment for homework and she coordinated a range of community-based activities for children, including youth projects and community service volunteers. Another project (the South Glamorgan Challenging Behaviour Project) provides a service for children whose behaviour has seriously 'challenged' everyone and provides a support team which coordinates assessment (with any service providers including schools, families, etc.) and which reviews the child's progress *with the child* on a monthly basis to ensure that he or she is aware of the plan, the objectives to be covered and can share in any progress monitoring. A third example of direct help for children and young people is through the growing numbers of children's rights officers, who are being appointed by local authorities to provide an independent voice for children and young people when they are 'looked after' by the local authority.

Creating positive learning environments with children

The OFSTED report (1994) *Access and Achievement in Urban Education* notes the impact of the environment 'outside the school gate', where there are multiple problems which adversely affect children's progress and participation and which cannot be tackled by teachers in planning children's futures. The same report emphasises the importance of involving children and young people in decision-making and also in supporting vulnerable families wherever possible so that they can participate more fully in education in its widest sense. The growth of the self-advocacy group for people with learning difficulties, People First, has clearly shown that even people with communication problems and severe learning difficulties *do* have clear images of themselves and may feel (albeit often unexpressed) discrimination and isolation as keenly as their peers.

David Jones (l993), writing about associated emotional difficulties experienced by children with learning difficulties or disabilities, emphasises the importance of acknowledging the special vulnerability of children with special needs – and the possibility that children with special needs may have incomplete understanding of a complex social world and the behaviours expected in order to survive within it. But he also emphasises the importance of developing coping strategies and acknowledging the possibility of change and development.

Parents have a special role to play in acknowledging their children's special needs – and their cognitive capacity so that they can reduce the causes of frustration and confusion for children. An extensive literature on the feeling of perceptions of parents of children with special needs has clearly shown both the capacity of parents to encourage positive attitudes in children with special needs – and also the emotional and physical pressures of providing such care. Sometimes listening to children may anger teachers and other professionals; not all parents wish to be 'partners'. Sadly not all parents (for a variety of reasons) are 'good enough' parents. If a child feels him or herself to have been abandoned by family or community, educational failure may simply seem one more failure in a disjointed and disrupted life.

David Galloway *et al.* (1982) quote a child who had been excluded from his local school after a period of aggressive behaviour, learning difficulties and trouble with the police. A research worker had asked the 15-year-old why he behaved like he did and succeeded in alienating the very people with whom he so badly needed to establish a good relationship. John's views of the world, his family and the so-called helping professionals were poignantly summed up:

> My mum said she hated the sight of me – and she said it in Court as well .... Every time I go to see her, she tells me to piss off home ... it was always me who got into trouble with the police. Our Dan didn't and our Ben didn't either. If I argue with my mother, our Ben hits me and if I argue with Ben, Dad hits me, so I can't win anyway. I asked to see Miss O again [an educational psychologist] but the deputy head said she was too busy. No one has time for you.

Without considerable support, this young person is unlikely to contribute positively to any school-based assessment. Unpopular with his peers, disruptive in class and disrupted by frequent break-downs in foster placements, he will require long-term support in order to achieve stability. But having stated his case with the school, he began to empower teachers and colleagues in turn to help him. His anger, bad language and behaviour become, in Martin Herbert's words, 'explainable', if not acceptable. Young people *can* learn to speak more powerfully for themselves before crisis occurs, if they are given the time and support within which to acquire such skills.

Micheline Mason (l981), writing about her realisation of the impact of her physical disability on her growth and development as a child, says:

> The first time the doubt that I belonged to this particular planet struck me, it was a glorious calm blue-skied day when I was twelve years old. Lying flat on my back in the garden, I was thinking about growing up. Until that moment, I think I had somehow believed that when I grew up, I would become 'normal', ie without a disability. 'Normal' then meant to me 'like my big sister', pretty, rebellious, going out with boys, leaving school, getting a job, leaving home, getting married, having children. That momentous day I suddenly realised that my life was not going to be like that at all. I was going to be just the same as I had always been – very small, funny shaped unable to walk. It seemed that at that moment the sky cracked ... my girl friend from next door came out and wanted a game as she had done many times before. I remember her look of confusion when I said I didn't want to play any more.

Micheline began the slow process of abandoning her 'handicapped identity':

> Animals have it easy. I mean for example it's very unlikely that a horse wastes much time wondering if she really is a horse, while human beings seem disposed to spend vast amounts of time wondering if they really are human beings at all. Well some do.

Micheline Mason, now Chair of the Integration Alliance, reminds us of the importance of disability equality training for all schools and the need to create and promote positive role models for children whose special needs may otherwise create lowered self-esteem and poor achievement.

Changing policy and practice in schools: what do children think?

David Jones (1993) underlines the importance of peer group relations for pupils with special needs – and the difficulties which may be encountered by children who look 'different'. What do *other* children think about fellow pupils with special educational needs? Ann Lewis (1991), in *Entitled to Learn Together*?, looks at a number of studies of the precise nature of interaction between so called 'normal' pupils and those with special educational needs. She notes a wide range of shared learning experiences in the best schools, including the use of 'buddies', peer tutoring, and collaborative learning. She found certain key themes in a wide range of studies which are of considerable importance in creating a positive climate of opinion towards children with special educational needs in a school setting:

1. When asked to describe their peers with severe learning difficulties, very few of the 'ordinary' children made any reference to their *lack* of ability. Overwhelmingly the children with special educational needs were described – like other children – in terms of their physical characteristics. 'Some have got brown eyes. Lucy has a red dress'.
2. The 'ordinary' children generally believed that when their peers with learning difficulties grew up, they too would have ordinary jobs like teachers, taxi drivers, etc.
3. However, the above belief was in some ways often linked to perceptions of the children with special needs as being 'young' and therefore going to 'grow out of it'. Older children needed some explanation in order to understand difficult behaviour or continued problems with learning. In effect they needed to have some real

understanding of the *internal* as well as *external* features of the children.

4. All children are different (with or without formally ascertained special needs). Including children with severe learning difficulties often contributed to awareness of the 'uniqueness' of individuals and was not a negative experience.

In effect, other children are part of the solution (as well as the problem) of unhappiness in their peer group, and it is clear that fellow pupils can share responsibility for supporting another pupil with a special educational need or disability.

What is clear from the Lewis study is that the 'ordinary' children can produce interesting 'enablers' who are adept at managing collaborative tasks with their partners with special needs. Anne Lewis (op. cit.) found no clear correlation between their skills and having previous experience of disability or of having younger siblings. The 'enablers' came from both sexes and included the less able children. But what they had in common was the ability to sequence and to work effectively on common tasks, drawing on different but complementary skills and avoiding dominance. We need to know more about 'enabling children' – not least because their skills could be utilised with a wider range of children who find life difficult or problematic.

In conclusion

Listening to children and young people with special educational needs or disabilities will present constant challenges. But it is also an opportunity for 'open learning' and a reminder that simplistic expectations about low participation rates and the inability to discuss sensitive issues in a positive way are often confounded. Both Part III of the 1993 Education Act and the Code of Practice confirm and amplify the key messages of the Children Act 1989, namely the right of children to be heard; the positive consequences of pupil involvement in addressing special educational needs; and the possibility of developing new partnerships with pupils to complement parent partnership and to ensure that the new approaches to meeting special educational needs as set out in the Code of Practice are understood, implemented and reinforced by all concerned. As one young woman with learning difficulties in the National Children's Bureau's self-advocacy project *Something to Say* (Wertheimer and Russell, in press) commented:

> We [pupils with special needs] want to let people know what we can do with our mouths, our hands, our brains. We want you to think about what we are saying, what we feel about things. It isn't easy. Don't turn your back on us and try to understand that lots of people on the street have difficulty in writing. Sometimes they treat us like zombies, like people from another planet. But we can speak for ourselves. We would like to do better. Treat us like human beings and we can all work together.

Working together with pupils and children will be the next challenge for the coming decade. It is a challenge – and an opportunity, if we tackle it optimistically.

Part IV

Conclusions

CHAPTER 10

A Way Forward?

David Galloway and Ron Davie

Introduction

It is odd to start the final chapter in a book on listening to children in education contexts by asking why it is desirable to do so. Yet the tension between different arguments for listening to the child's point of view has been a recurring theme in previous chapters. In our opening chapter we quoted the head of a primary school as saying: '... giving children a say in policy made it more difficult for them to object'.

Marion Bennathan's chapter, too, draws attention to the pragmatic value of projects which give children a greater sense of ownership over decisions affecting them. These pragmatic arguments are very different from the legal requirement embodied in the Code of Practice (DfE, 1994a), the moral case argued, from different perspectives, by both Freeman and Russell, and the curriculum case developed by Marland and Griffiths. The legal requirements and pragmatic benefits can all too easily obscure the moral and educational arguments: 'The last temptation, it is the greatest treason: To do the right thing for the wrong reason' (from T.S. Eliot, *Murder in the Cathedral*).

The obstacles to a 'listening culture' are formidable. Griffiths drew attention to the increasing pressures on schools, and Armstrong and Galloway to the structural difficulties in extending the concept of partnership to children in the assessment of their special educational needs. We will not develop a listening culture in schools by urging teachers to take on new tasks, which they may well see as marginal to their mainstream work at a time when they already feel under pressure. Nor will it help to urge that school effectiveness research demonstrates the importance of recognising children's perspectives. It is not clear whether teachers are able to listen to children's viewpoints because their school is successful, or whether it is successful at least partly because teachers listen. Moreover, the application of school effectiveness research in school improvement projects is fraught with difficulty.

What is needed is a coherent *educational* rationale for listening to the voice of the child based on teachers' mainstream work. In this chapter we summarise the grounds for optimism and pessimism described in previous chapters and explore the nebulous but important notion of 'good practice'. We shall review the cognitive and affective aspects of listening, and conclude by arguing that progress requires building on teachers' existing skills, rather than asking them to acquire new ones.

Optimism or pessimism?

In asking if there are grounds for optimism we need to look at the range of activities included in a 'listening culture'. Clearly, a listening culture has implications both for curriculum content and for pedagogy. Listening is a two-way process requiring encouragement to express ideas and feelings as well as responsiveness to them. Marland's analysis of the 1988 Education Reform Act and Griffiths' of OHMCI's (1994a) working papers for school inspections offer grounds for optimism. For the first time, communication skills have been incorporated into the curriculum at a national level, with active support from the inspectorate. Indeed, OFSTED appears to be moving beyond the formal requirements of the National Curriculum by encouraging pupils' involvement in school councils and similar activities. Systematic policies for obtaining and acting on feedback from students are already a requirement in initial teacher training, and increasingly are likely to be expected as part of school quality assurance mechanisms.

Twenty years ago few HMI reports made more than a cursory reference to pastoral care or personal and social education; today they invariably receive close attention from OFSTED. Similarly, exclusion rates were seldom recorded, and that, too, has changed. A cynic might claim that pastoral care is now the subject of official attention not because it is seen as an important aspect of a 'listening school' but because its quality is deteriorating. Griffiths argues that this is attributable to the pressures created by the reforms of the last 15 years. Paradoxically, while parts of the National Curriculum may be moving towards the ideal of a listening school, with OFSTED's active support, the hidden curriculum may be moving in the opposite direction. Exclusion rates appear to be rising (Advisory Centre for Education, 1993) and the 1993 Education Act framework for the assessment of special educational needs was clearly motivated less by a commitment to strengthen the child's role in assessment than by administrative problems arising from the 1981 Act. Interestingly, the 1993 Act, like the 1981 Act, embodies a broad professional consensus on what constitutes 'good practice', and we need to look more closely at this concept to see if it can offer a way through the paradox.

'Good practice'

Superficially, good practice in listening to the child's voice in schools is seen in:

- a curriculum which develops sharing and communication of knowledge, understanding and attitudes;
- a pastoral care system which is responsive to 'normal' needs, for example transition to secondary school or choice of GCSE subjects, and to exceptional or special needs;
- structures which enable teachers to find out and respond to how pupils perceive the curriculum and school or classroom organisation.

Yet each of these is culturally loaded. In many countries the curriculum is assessed almost exclusively in terms of paper and pencil tests; encouraging the sharing of ideas is not part of the teacher's job. Similarly, the time spent on pastoral care in Britain bewilders teachers from many countries, who see their job as teaching, not counselling or social work. Nor do the criteria for good practice listed above tell us *why* listening to children's viewpoints is desirable.

Pragmatic reasons cannot be adequate. Would we say that listening to children was unnecessary if the evidence did *not* so clearly show that it improved relationships? The notion of good practice is inextricably linked to the aims of education and these are based on the values of those who hold them, whether teachers, administrators or politicians. Were that not so, there might be greater consensus between the teaching profession and the government. In other words, the aims of education are concerned with moral and political priorities, and if this argument is correct, criteria for good practice should depend on whose priorities we are talking about. Surprisingly, though, people with widely different moral and political priorities agree on the importance of a listening culture even though they disagree on the reasons for its importance. A liberal perspective is likely to see listening to children as desirable *prima facie*. A more instrumental view might be based on British children's poor performance in international comparisons (e.g., Prais, 1986), particularly with respect to those pupils referred to by the late Lord Joseph as 'the bottom 40 per cent'. This leads to concerns about our ability to compete in international markets; it offers a justification for the demand for higher standards and curriculum reform leading to more 'transferable skills'. By definition, though, teaching transferable skills requires an interactive pedagogy which in turn implies responsiveness to pupils' perceptions and experience

Cognitive and affective aspects of listening

There is no need to spend time on the outdated view that the official or National Curriculum is concerned principally with cognitive aspects of listening and communication while the pastoral system is concerned with affective aspects. The curriculum, obviously, does aim to develop communication and listening skills, but these have both cognitive and affective elements. Similarly, as Marland (1980) has argued, the pastoral curriculum is concerned with pupils' knowledge and understanding as well as with their personal and social welfare.

Communication and listening are as important in children's intellectual development as in their emotional and social development. In this sense communication and listening are skills which the academic and pastoral curriculum should be developing in pupils, as well as skills which the school's professional development programme may need to develop in teachers. To see whether or not a review of the latter is needed, we have to consider two questions. Both feature prominently in the critical literature on pastoral care (e.g., Best *et al.*, 1980).

First, is it possible for teachers to encourage communication and listening within the classroom, but not in other areas of school life, such as implementation of policies on discipline, and pastoral care? In theory, the question could be said to show a misunderstanding of the relationships between these policies and the curriculum, with the former existing to promote effective teaching of the latter. According to this argument, effective teaching is interactive and involves seeking, listening to and valuing children's experience; it involves a way of interacting with children which cannot stop at the classroom door. In practice this is at best an oversimplification and at worst plainly wrong. Children change their behaviour instantly, effortlessly and often almost unconsciously as the context changes. To see this, one only has to observe how they behave in different ways with different teachers. The same can be true of teachers. Pastoral heads of year may be sensitive, 'listening' teachers of, say, English, but when dealing with disciplinary problems in their pastoral role – a situation which may be regrettable but is certainly common – they can become inflexible in defending the status quo and in supporting their colleagues.

This leads to the second question: is it possible to encourage communication and listening with some children but not with others? In principle it clearly *is* possible. Williamson's (1980) analysis of pastoral care argues that only the brightest and most successful pupils receive an enabling variety of pastoral care. The rest are 'pastoralised' into accepting a restricted range of opportunities. Williamson's argument brings us back to the purpose of listening. Ideally, it is to help the school adapt to the needs of its pupils. All too easily it can become a none-too-subtle form of social control designed to prop up an unsatisfactory status quo.

Conclusions

Building on existing skills

The central implication of our argument is thus that listening requires a policy which extends to all aspects of a school's work. However, it cannot be assumed that teachers who encourage and enable children to talk in one context will be able to do so in another context. Nor can it be assumed that all pupils will receive the same encouragement to talk, let alone for the same reasons. It is, nevertheless, clear not only that effective teaching requires seeking, listening to and valuing the child's experience, but also that a characteristic of effective schools is the high level of consistency between teachers (e.g., Mortimore *et al*., 1988).

Hence, in building a listening school, the emphasis should be on developing teachers' skills *as teachers*, not on expecting them to acquire new skills, for example in counselling. That said, although teachers should not try to act as counsellors, they do require some counselling skills. For example, talking to parents about a child's learning or behavioural difficulties or talking to an individual child about non-completed homework can elicit information about complex family matters, requiring a sensitive response. Similarly, creating a 'safe' environment in the classroom and outside it which allows children to express personally sensitive feelings or information requires high-level teaching skills, which overlap with the interpersonal skills required of counsellors. It is not hard to find other examples. The teaching skill of ending a lesson successfully has something in common with the counsellor's or psychotherapist's skill of closing an interview. An interpretation in psychotherapy has something in common with a skilled teacher's ability to give a hint which enables a child or group of children to reach the solution to a problem. Yet although there is common ground, the starting point is the teacher's ability *as a teacher*. Both for teachers and for pupils, this is crucial. It is crucial for teachers because they cannot be expected to learn a new language and new skills at a time of unparalleled change. It is crucial for pupils because the school is a social institution plays such an important part in their lives (see Hargreaves, 1982). It is when they feel valued in the school's mainstream activities that pupils feel able to share anxieties about other aspects of their lives. It is when their suggestions about teaching methods and school organisation are sought that teachers can create what Hopkins *et al.* (1994) call the 'moving' school, which they see as:

> an ideal type of school which has achieved a healthy blend of change and stability, and [has] balanced development and maintenance. Internally the school is relatively calm as it adapts successfully to an often rapidly changing environment (p.91).

They contrast 'moving schools' with 'wandering', 'stuck' or 'promenading schools'.

In creating a listening culture we are talking about far more than the school's contribution to the welfare of a troubled minority of pupils, important though that is. We are talking about how teachers become more effective in the education of *all* their pupils by recognising and responding to what their pupils tell them.

References

Acland, T. (1902) *Memoir and Letters of The Right Honourable Sir Thomas Dyke Acland*, A. Acland (ed.), privately printed, London.

Advisory Centre for Education (1993) *Findings from the ACE Investigation into Exclusions*, London: ACE.

Alexander, R. (1992) *Policy and Practice in Primary Education.*, London: Routledge.

Alexander, R., Rose, J. and Woodhead, C. (1992) *Curriculum Organisation and Classroom Practice in Primary Schools: A Discussion Paper*, London: DES.

Alford, H. (1873) *Life, Journal and Letters of Henry Alford, DD.*, F. Alford (ed.), London: Rivingtons.

Anderson, R. D. (1983) *Education and Opportunity in Victorian Scotland. Schools and Universities*, Oxford: Clarendon Press.

The Archbishop of Canterbury's Commission on Urban Priority Areas (1985) *Faith in the City*, London: Church House Publishing.

Armstrong, D. and Galloway, D. (1992) 'Who is the child psychologist's client? Responsibilities and options for psychologists in educational settings', *Association for Child Psychology and Psychiatry Newsletter*, 14 (2) 62–66.

Armstrong, D., Galloway, D. and Tomlinson, S. (1993) 'The assessment of special educational needs and the proletarianisation of professionals', *British Journal of Sociology of Education*, 14 (4) 399–408.

Association of Metropolitan Authorities (1995) *Reviewing Special Educational Needs*, London: AMA.

Audit Commission (1994) *Seen But Not Heard*, London: Audit Commission.

Bannister, A., Barrett, K. and Shearer, E. (1990)(Eds.) *Listening to Children: The Professional Response to Hearing the Abused Child*, London: Longman for NSPCC.

Barber, M. (1994) *Young People and Their Attitudes to School*, Keele: Centre for Successful Schools, Keele University.

Barbiana, School of (1969) *Letter to a Teacher*, Harmonsworth: Penguin.

Bargh, J. (1990) *The Friday Afternoon Book*, London: National Children's Bureau.

Barsby, J. (1991) 'Self evaluation and seven year olds', *Education 3–13*, 19, 1, 12–17.

Bazalgette, J. (1982) *Taking Up The Pupil Role*, London: The Grubb Institute.

Bean, P. and Melville, J. (1989) *Lost Children of the Empire*, London: Unwin Hyman.

Bernstein, B. (1973) 'Education cannot compensate for society', 1n J. Raynor and J. Harde (eds) *Equality and City Schools. Readings in Urban Education, Vol.2*, London: Routledge. Kegan Paul in association with Open University.

Best, R., Jarvis, C. and Ribbins, P. (eds)(1980) *Perspectives on Pastoral Care*, London: Heinemann.

Blatchford, P. (1992) 'Academic self-assessment at 7 and 11 years: Its accuracy and association with ethnic group and sex', *British Journal of Educational Psychology*, 62, 35–44.

Blatchford, P. and Sharp, S. (1994) *Breaktime and the School*, London: Routledge.

Bolger, A.W. (1975) *Child Study and Guidance in Schools*, London: Constable.

Boud, D. (1992) 'The use of self-assessment in negotiated learning', *Studies in Higher Education*, 17 (2) 185–200.

Bower, A.C. (1903) *The Diaries and Correspondence of Anna Catherina Bower*, privately printed, London.

Bowlby, J. (1953) *Child Care and the Growth of Love*, London: Pelican Books.

Braithwaite, A. (1905) *Memoirs of Anna Braithwaite*, J.B. Braithwaite (ed.), London: Headley Brothers.

Bridgeland, M. (1971) *Pioneer Work with Maladjusted Children*, London: Staples.

Bright, J. (1930) *Diaries of John Bright*, R. Walling (ed.), London: Cassell.

Broadfoot, P. (ed.)(1986) *Profiles and Records of Achievement: A Review of Issues and Practices*, London: Holt, Rinehart and Winston.

Broughton, V. D. (ed.) (1887) *Court and Private Life in the Time of Queen Charlotte: Being the Journals of Mrs Papendiek, Assistant Keeper of the Wardrobe and Reader to her Majesty*, London: Richard Bentley, 2 vols.

Burns, R. (1982) *Self-Concept Development and Education*, New York: Holt, Reinhart and Winston.

Butler-Sloss, E. (1988) *Report of the Inquiry into Child Abuse in Cleveland in 1987*, London: HMSO.

CACE (1967) *Children and their Primary Schools* (The Plowden Report), London: HMSO.

Chittenden, A. (1993) 'How can a pastoral care programme improve a school culture', *Pastoral Care in Education*, 11 (3) 29–35.

Cohen, L. (ed.) (1935) *Lady de Rothschild and her Daughters, 1821–1931*, London: John Murray.

Cooper, A. (1886) *The Life and Work of the 7th Earl of Shaftesbury*, E. Hodder, London: Cassell & Co., 3 vols.

Cooper, P. (1993a) *Equality and City Schools: Readings in Urban Education*, Vol. 2, London: Routledge and Kegan Paul in association with the Open University Press.

Cooper, P. (1993b) 'Improving the behaviour and academic performance of pupils through the Curriculum', *Educational Review*, 29 (4) 255–66.

Cooper, P. (1993c) 'Learning from pupils' perspectives', *British Journal of Special Education*, 20, 4, 129–33

Cowie, H. (1994) 'Ways of involving children in decision making', in P. Blatchford and S. Sharp (eds) *Breaktime and the School*, London: Routledge.

Cox, B. (1985) *The Law of Special Educational Needs: A Guide to the Education Act 1981*, Beckenhau: Croom Helm.

Cox, C.B. and Boyson, R. (1977) *Black Paper 1977*. London: Maurice Temple Smith.

Cronk, K.A. (1987) *Teacher-Pupil Conflict in Secondary Schools*, London: Falmer Press.

David, K. and Charlton, T. (in press) Pastoral Care Matters: In Primary and Middle Schools, London: Routledge.

Davie, R. (1989) 'The National Children's Bureau: Evidence to the Elton Committee', in N. Jones (ed.) *School Management and Pupil Behaviour*, London: Falmer Press.

Davie, R. (1993) 'Listen to the child: a time for change', *The Psychologist*, 6, (June) 252–7.

Davie, R. (1994) 'A consortium for children: analysis of the dialogue with policy makers leading to the 1993 Education Act and the 1994 Code of Practice', *Therapeutic Care and Education*, 3 (3) 206–17.

Davie, R., Phillips, D. and Callely, E. (1984) *Evaluation of INSET Course on Behaviour Problems. Report to Welsh Office*, Cardiff: Department. of Education, University College.

de Leo, M. (1994) 'Selecting Secondry Schools', personal communication.

Department for Education (1992) *Choice and Diversity: A New Framework for Schools*, London: HMSO.

Department for Education (1994a) *Code of Practice on the Identification and Assessment of Special Educational Needs*, London: DfE.

Department for Education (1994b) *Exclusions From School: Circular 10/94*, London: DfE.

Department for Education (1994c) *Pupils with Problems: Circular 9/94 The Education of Children with Emotional and Behavioural Difficulties; Circular 8/94 Pupil Behaviour and Discipline; Circular 13/94 Children Looked After by the Local Authority*, London: DfE.

Department of Education and Science (1978) *Special Educational Needs* (The Warnock Report), London: HMSO.

Department of Education and Science (1982) *Experience and Participation: Report of the Review Group on the Youth Service in England (The Thompson Report)*, London: HMSO.

Department of Education and Science (1988) *The Education Reform Act*, London: HMSO.

Department of Education and Science (1989a) *Assessments and Statements of Special Educational Needs: Procedures within the Education, Health and Social Services* (Circular 22/89) London: DES.

Department of Education and Science (1989b) *Discipline in Schools* (The Elton Report), London: Department of Education and Science.

Department of Education and Science (1989c) *Records of Achievement National Steering Committee Report*, London: HMSO.

Department of Health (1992) The Children Act Guidance and Regulations: Volume 6, *Children with Disabilities*, London: HMSO.

Dewey, J. (1900) *The School and Society*, Chicago: University of Chicago Press.

Dryden manuscripts. Curriculum for Frank, D(CA) 283; Northampton Record Office.

Epps, J. (1875) *Diary of the Late John Epps*, E. Epps (ed.), London: Kent & Co.

Fleming, M. (1934) *The Complete Marjory Fleming*, F. Sidgwick (ed.), London: Sidgwick & Jackson.

Francis, H. (1993) *Teachers Listening to Learners' Voices*, British Psychological Society Education Section, Leicester: BPS.

Galloway, D. Ball, T., Blomfield, D. and Seyd, R. (1982) *Schools and Disruptive Pupils*. London: Longman.

Galloway, D. (1990) *Pupil Welfare and Counselling: An Approach to Personal and Social Education Across the Curriculum*, London: Longman.

Galloway, D., Armstrong, D. and Tomlinson, S. (1994) *The Assessment of Special Educational Needs: Whose Problem?*, London: Longman.

Gardner, P. (1984) *The Lost Elementary Schools of Victorian England*, Beckenham: Croom Helm.

Gardner, R. (1987) *Who Says? Choice and Control in Care*, London: NCB.

Garner, P. (1992) 'Involving "disruptive" students in school discipline structures', *Pastoral Care in Education*, 10 (3) 13–19.

Gaskell, J. (1883) *Records of an Eton Schoolboy*, C. Gaskell (ed.), privately printed, London.

Gathorne-Hardy, J. (1977) *The Public School Phenomenon*, London: Hodder Stoughton.

Gersch, I. (1987) 'Involving pupils in their own assessment', in T. Bowers (ed.) *Special Educational Needs and Human Resource Management*, Beckenham: Croom Helm.

Gersch, I.S. (1990) 'The pupils' view', in M. Scherer, I.S. Gersch and L. Fry (eds) *Meeting Disruptive Behaviour, Assessment, Interaction and Partnerships*, Basingstoke: Macmillan.

Gersch, I. (1994) *Working Together for Children and Young People: The Student Report*, London Borough of Waltham Forest, Department of Educational Psychology.

Gersch, I. (in press) 'Educational perspectives', in R. Davie, G. Upton and V. Varma (eds) *The voice of the Child: A Handbook for Professionals*, London: Fulton.

Gillick (1986) *Gillick v West Norfolk and Wisbech Area Health Authority*, 1 FLR 224.

Goldstrom, J. M. (1972) *Education: Elementary Education 1870–1900*, Newton Abbot: David & Charles.

Gore, J. (1935) *Nelson's Hardy and His Wife, 1769–1877*, London: John Murray.

Gosden, P.H.J.H. (1969) *How They Were Taught. An Anthology of Contemporary Accounts of Learning and Teaching in England 1800–1950*, New York: Barnes & Noble.

Guest, C. (1950) *Lady Charlotte Guest. Extracts from Her Journal 1833–52*, Earl of Bessborough (ed.), London: John Murray.

Haldane, M. (1925) *A Record of a Hundred Years 1825–1925*, her daughter (ed.), London: Hodder & Stoughton.

Hargreaves, D. (1982) *The Challenge for the Comprehensive School: Culture, Curriculum and Community*, London: Routledge and Kegan Paul.

Hargreaves, D. (1984) *Improving Secondary Schools*, London: Inner London Education Authority.

Harrop, A. and Holmes, M. (1993) 'Teachers' perceptions of their pupils' views on rewards and punishments', *Pastoral Care in Education*, 11 (1) 30–35.

Harvey, W. (1936) *We Were Seven*, London: Constable & Co.

Head, C. (1905) 'Diary of Caroline Head', in C. Hanbury, *Life of Mrs Albert Head*, London: Marshall Brothers, pp. 42–160.

Heber manuscripts. English Letters, C. 203; Bodleian Library.
Hegarty, S. (1981) *Educating Pupils with Special Educational Needs in the Ordinary School*, Windsor: NFER-Nelson.
Hendrick, H. (1992) 'Children and childhood', *ReFRESH*, No. 15, Autumn.
HMI (1992) *The New Teacher in School*, a survey by HM Inspectors in England and Wales 1992, London: Office of Her Majesty's Chief Inspector of Schools.
HMI (1994) *Framework for the Inspection of Schools, Revised May 1994*, London: Office for Standards in Education.
Hodgkin, R. (1993) 'Pupils' views and the Education Bill', *Concern*, 86, 8–9.
Hodgkin, R. (1994) 'The right to consent to treatment', *Children UK*, 3, 4–5.
Hooper, J. (1994) *'Speaking Proper': Accent, Dialect and Identity*, Southampton: Centre for Language in Education, Southampton University.
Hopkins, D., Ainscow, M. and West, D. (1994) *School Improvement in an Era of Change*, London: Cassell.
Hopkins, E. (1994) *Childhood Transformed. Working-Class Children in Nineteenth-Century England*, Manchester: Manchester University Press.
Horn, P. (1980) 'The recruitment, role and status of the Victorian Country teacher', *History of Education*, Vol. 9, pp. 129–41.
Horn, P. (1989) 'The Victorian Governess' '*History of Education*' 18, 333-44.
Houston, R. A. (1988) *Literacy in Early Modern Europe. Culture & Education 1500–1800*, Harlow: Longman.
Hughes, K. (1993) *The Victorian Governess*, RioGrande, OH: Hambledon.
Humphreys, M. (1994) *Empty Cradles*, London: Doubleday.
Hurt, J. (1971) *Education in Evolution. Church, State, Society and Popular Education 1800–1870*; London: Rupert Hart-Davis.
James, J., Charlton, T., Leo, E. and Indoe, D. (1992) 'A peer to listen', *Support for Learning*, 6 (4) 165–9.
Jeune, M. D. (1932) *Pages from the Diary of an Oxford Lady*; M. Gifford (ed.), Oxford: Shakespeare Head Press.
Johnson, T.J. (1972) *Professions and Power*, Basingstoke: Macmillan.
Johnston, P. (1862) *Extracts from Priscilla Johnston's Journal*; E. MacInnes (ed.), Carlisle: Charles Thurnam & Sons.
Jones, D. (1993) 'Coping with unhappy children who have learning difficulties', in V. Varma (ed.) *Coping with Unhappy Children*, London: Cassell.
Jones, W. (1929) *The Diary of the Reverend William Jones*; O.F. Christie (ed.), London: Brentanos.
Jordan, E. (1991) '"Making good wives and mothers"? The transformation of middle-class girls' education in nineteenth-century Britain', *History of Education Quarterly*, Vol. 31, pp. 439–62.
Keegan, G. (1994) 'Raising the standard', in *Achievement and Under-achievement in Secondary Schools in Wales: OHMCI Conference Report*, 15–19.
Kerfoot, M. and Butler, A. (1988) *Problems of Childhood and Adolescence*, London: Routledge and Kegan Paul.
Keys, W. and Fernandes, C. (1993) *What do Students Think about School?*, Slough: NFER.
Kyriacou, C. (1986) *Effective Teaching in Schools*, Oxford: Blackwell.
Kyriacou, C. and Butcher, B. (1993) 'Stress in Year 11 school children', *Pastoral Care in Education*, 11 (3) 19–21.
Laqueur, T. (1976) 'Working-class demand and the growth of English elementary education, 1750–1850', In L. Stone (ed.) *Schooling and Society. Studies in the History of Education*, London: John Hopkins University Press, pp. 192–205.
Laslett, R. (1995) 'Beliefs and practice in the early schools for maladjusted pupils', *Therapeutic Care and Education*, V 4, 1, 5–8.
Lawrence, D. (1971) 'The effects of counselling on retarded readers', *Educational Research*, 13 (2) 119–24.

Lawrence, D. (1972) 'Counselling of retarded readers by non-professionals', *Educational Research*, 15 (1) 48–54.

Leach, P. (1990) 'Towards a child-friendly society', in A. Bannister, K. Barrett and E. Shearer (eds) *Listening to Children: the Professional Response to Hearing the Abused Child*, London: Longman.

Leach, P. (1994) *Children First*, London: Michael Joseph.

Lewis, A. (1991) 'Entitled to learn together?', in R. Ashdown, B. Carpenter and K. Bouvair (eds) *The Curriculum Challenge*, London: Falmer Press.

Lewis, A. (1988) 'Young children's attitudes, after a period of integration, towards peers with severe learning difficulties', *European Journal of Special Needs Education*, 3 (3) 161–72.

Lucas, W. (1934) A Quaker Journal; G.E. Bryant and G.P. Baker (eds), London: Hutchinson & Co.

Lynn, M. and Peel, E.A. (1977) 'A cognitive dimension in the analysis of classroom discourse', *Educational Review*, 29, 4, 255–66.

McIlvain, A. (1992) 'Quality speaks for itself', *Child Education*, March, 69 (3) 52–3.

McKelvey, J. and Kyriacou, C. (1985) 'Research on pupils as teacher evaluators', *Educational Studies*, 11, 25–31.

McMurray, P. (1986) 'Self-esteem and behaviour in school', in T. Charlton, H. Lambley and K. Jones (eds) *Educating Children with Learning and Behaviour Problems: Some Considerations*, Faculty of Education Monograph No. 1, Cheltenham: College of St. Paul and St. Mary Press.

Maher, P. (1987)(Ed.) *Child Abuse, The Educational Perspective*, Oxford: Basil Blackwell for the National Association for Pastoral Care in Education.

Marland, M. (1974) *Pastoral Care*. London: Heinemann.

Marland, M. (1980) 'The pastoral curriculum', in Best *et al*, *Perspectives on Pastoral Care*, London: Heinemann School Management Series.

Marland, M. (1989a) *The Tutor and the Tutor Group*, Harlow: Longman.

Marland, M. (1990) 'Telling tales: In and out of school', in A. Bannister, K. Barrett and E. Shearer (eds) *Listening to Children*, Harlow: Longman for the NSPCC.

Marland, M. (1995) 'The whole Curriculum', in R. Best, P. Lang, C. Lodge and C. Watkins (eds) *Pastoral Care and Personal Social Education: Entitlement and Provision*, London: Cassell.

Marland M. (Gen. Ed) (1989b) *Longman Tutorial Resources* (six books), London: Longman.

Mason, M. (1981) 'Finding a voice', in J. Campling (ed.) *Images of Ourselves: Women with Disabilities Talking*, London: Routledge and Kegan Paul.

Mehrabian, A. (1972) *Silent Messages*, Belmont, CA: Wadsworth.

Melissa: A PGCE Student (1992) 'Being at the receiving end', *Pastoral Care in Education*, 8 (4) 16–19.

Mill, J. (1889) 'The diary of the Reverend John Mill', G. Goudie (ed.), *Scottish History Society*, Vol. 5.

Mitford, N. (ed.) (1938) *The Ladies of Alderley being the Letters Between Maria Josepha, Lady Stanley of Alderley and her Daughter-in-law Henrietta Maria Stanley During the Years 1841-50*; London: Chapman & Hall.

Mortimore, P., Sammons, P., Stoll, L., Lewis, D. and Ecob, R. (1988) *School Matters: The Junior Years*, Wells: Open Books.

Morton, J. (1994) *Involving the Child: Code of Practice School-Based Assessment: Teachers Pack*, Kingston-upon-Thames: Surrey CC.

Murfitt, J. and Thomas, J.B. (1983) 'The effects of peer counselling on the self-concept and reading attainment of secondary aged slow learning pupils', *Remedial Education*, 18 (2) 73–4.

Murphy, R. and Torrance, H. (1988) *The Changing Face of Assessment*, Buckingham: Open University Press.

Nabuzoka, D. *et al*. (1993) 'Bullying and children with special needs in school', in D. Tattum (ed.) *Understanding and Managing Bullying*, London: Heinemann.

Naish, J. (1994) 'Children in the Health Service', *Children Act News*, April, p.3, London: Department of Health.
National Children's Bureau (1990) *The Friday Book*, London: NCB.
National Children's Bureau (1994) 'Listening to children', *Concern*, 88, 3.
Office of Her Majesty's Chief Inspector of Schools (Wales) (1994a) *Handbook for the Inspection of Schools*, Wrexham.
Office of Her Majesty's Chief Inspector of Schools in Wales (1994a) *Achievement and Under-Achievement*, Conference Report, Cardiff.
OFSTED (1994) *Access and Achievement in Urban Education*, London: OFSTED/HMSO.
OFSTED (1995a) *New Framework for the Inspection of Schools*, London: HMSO.
OFSTED (1994b) *The Annual Report of Her Majesty's Chief Inspector of Schools*, London: HMSO.
Owen, I.R. (1991) 'Using the sixth sense: the place and relevance of language in counselling', *British Journal of Guidance and Counselling*, 19 (3) 307–19.
Owenson, S. (1863) *Lady Morgan's Memoirs*, ed. D.W. Hepworth, London: W.H.Allen.
Page, R. and Clarke, G.A. (1977) (eds) *Who Cares? Children in Care Speak Out*, London: NCB.
Parker, J.O. (1964) *The Oxley Parker Papers*; Colchester: Benham & Co.
Parsons, C. (1994) *Excluding Primary School Children*, London: Family Policy Studies Centre.
Peagram, E. and Upton, G. (1991) 'Emotional and behavioural difficulties and the Elton Report', *Maladjustment and Therapeutic Education*, 9 (1) 41–8.
Pease, E. (1907) *The Diaries of Edward Pease*; A. Pease (ed.), London: Headley Brothers.
Pedersen, J.S. (1975) 'Schoolmistresses and headmistresses: elites and education in nineteenth-century England', *Journal of British Studies*, Vol. 15, pp. 135–62.
Peterson, M.J. (1973) 'The Victorian governess: status incongruence in family and society', in M. Vicinus (ed.) *Suffer and Be Still. Women in the Victorian Age*, Bloomington and London: Indiana University Press, pp. 3–19.
Pigot, T. (1989) *Report of the Advisory Group on Video Recorded Evidence*, London: Home Office.
Pollen, J. (1912) *John Hungerford Pollen*, A. Polen (ed.), London: John Murray.
Pollock, L.A. (1983) *Forgotten Children. Parent-child Relations from 1500 to 1900*, Cambridge: Cambridge University Press.
Prais, S. (1986) 'Educating for productivity: comparisons of Japanese and English schooling and vocational preparation', *Compare*, 16 (ii), 121–47.
Preston, B. (1995) 'Head teachers Could Face Appraisal by their Staff', *The Times*, 21 February, 8.
Purvis, J. (1989) *Hard Lessons. The Lives and Education of Working-Class Women in Nineteenth-century England*, Minneapolis: University of Minnesota Press.
Quarmby, D. (1993) 'Peer group counselling with bereaved adolescents', *British Journal of Guidance and Counselling*, 21 (2) 196–211.
Rames, M.L. (1911) 'Marie Louise Rames' Journal', in H.G. Huntington *Memories, Personages, Peoples, Places*; London: Constable & Co. pp. 228–96.
Ribbins, P. (ed.) (1985) *Schooling and Welfare*, London: Falmer.
Roach, J. (1986) 'Boy and girls at school, 1800-1870', *History of Education*, Vol. 15, pp. 147–59.
Rogers, C. (1951) *Client-Centred Therapy*, Boston: Houghton Mifflin.
Rogers, C. (1983) *Freedom to Learn: for the 80's*, New York: Macmillan.
Rosenbaum, M. and Newell, P. (1991) *Taking Children Seriously: A Proposal for a Children's Rights Commissioner*, London: Calouste Gulbenkian Foundation.
Ross, E. (1990) 'Learning to listen to children', in E. Bannister, K. Barnett and E. Shearer (eds) *Listening to Children*, London: Longman.
Rowe, J. (1982) *Yours by Choice: A Guide for Adoptive Parents*, London: Routledge and Kegan Paul.

Rule, R. (1992) *Albion's People. English Society 1714–1815*, Harlow: Longman.
Russell, B. and P. (eds) (1966) *The Amberley Papers*; London: George Allen & Unwin, 2 vols.
Rutter, M., Maughan, B., Mortimore, P. and Ouston, J. (1979) *Fifteen Thousand House*, London: Open Books.
Sandford, D. (1830) *Remains of the Late Right Reverend Daniel Sandford*; Edinburgh: Waugh & Innes, 2 vols.
Screech, M.A. (1983) *Montaigne and Melancholy*, London: Duckworth.
Sebba, J. (1983) 'Social interventions among pre-school handicapped and non-handicapped children', *Journal of Mental Deficiency Research*, 17, 115–24.
Sewell, E. (1907) *The Autobiography of Elizabeth Sewell*; E. Sewell (ed), London: Longmans, Green & Co.
Sharp, S. and Blatchford, P. (1994) 'Understanding and changing school breaktime behaviour: themes and conclusions', in P. Blatchford and S. Sharp (eds) *Breaktime and the School*, London: Routledge.
Sharp, S. and Smith, P.K. (1991) 'Bullying in school: the DfE Sheffield Bullying Project', *Early Child Development and Care*, 77, 47–55.
Sharp, S., Sellars, A. and Cowie, H. (1994) 'Time to listen: setting up a peer counselling service to tackle the problem of bullying in school', *Pastoral Care in Education*, 12 (2) 3–6.
Shelley, F. (1912) *The Diary of Frances, Lady Shelley*; R. Edgcumbe (ed.), London: John Murray, 2 vols.
Short, P. (1993) 'Integration. The Perception of Parents and Staff of the Integration of Children with Particular Special Needs into a Mainstream Comprehensive School', unpublished Adv. Dip. Dissertation, University of Wales.
Smith, P.M. (in press) 'Social work perspective', in R. Davie, G. Upton and V. Varma (eds) *The Voice of the Child: A Handbook for Professionals*, London: Fulton.
Smith, S. (1953) *The Letters of Sydney Smith*; N. Smith (ed.), Oxford: Clarendon Press, 2 vols.
Special Educational Needs Tribunal (1994) *Special Educational Needs Tribunal: How to Appeal*, London: SENT.
Spencer, J. (1990) *The Evidence of Children – the Law and the Psychology*, London: Blackburn Press.
SSI (1994) *Services to Disabled Children and Their Families: Report of the National Inspection of Services and Disabled Children and Their Families*, London: HMSO.
Statham, J. (1987) 'Speaking for ourselves – self-advocacy for people with learning difficulties', in *Including Pupils with Disabilities: A Curriculum for All*, Buckingham: Open University Press.
Steadman, T. (1838) *Memoir of William Steadman*; London: Thomas Ward & Co.
Sweetingham, P. and Woods, L. (1994) 'Supporting tuturoing implications for pastoral care', *Pastoral Care in Education*, 12, 1, 3–9.
Times Educational Supplement (1992) 'Children claim the right to choose', 26 June, Primary News.
Times Educational Supplement (1994) 'Where children write the rules', 21 January, p.13.
Towler, L. and Broadfoot, P. (1992) 'Self-assessment in the primary school', *Educational Review*, 44 (2) 137–51.
Townsend, J. (1828) *Memoirs of the Reverend John Townsend*; London: J. B. & John Courthope.
Trench, M. (1862) *The Remains of the Late Mrs Trench*; Dean of Westminster (ed.), London: Parker, Son, & Bourn.
Vulliamy, G. and Webb, R. (1991) 'Teacher research and educational change: an empirical study', *British Educational Research Journal*, 17, 219–36.
Wade, B. and Moore, M. (1993) *Experiencing Special Education*, Buckingham: Open University Press.
Wade, B. and Moore, M. (1994) 'Good for a change? The views of students with special educational needs on changing school', *Pastoral Care in Education*, 12 (2) 23–7.

Walker, J. (1995) *The Cost of Communication Breakdown*, London: British Telecom.

Walvin, J. (1982) *A Child's World. A Social History of English Childhood 1800-1914*; Harmondsworth: Penguin.

Wertheimer, A. and Russell, P. (in press) Something to Say? New Approaches to Working with Group-work with Young Women with Learning Difficulties, London: National Children's Bureau.

Wheldall, K. and Merrett, F. (1982) *Batpack Positive Products*, Birmingham: University of Birmingham.

Whitwell, T. (1927) 'A Darlington schoolboy's diary', *The Journal of the Friends' Historical Society*, Vol. 24, pp. 21–30.

Williamson, D. (1980) '"Pastoral care" or "pastoralisation"?', in R. Best, C. Jarvis and P. Ribbins (eds) *Perspectives on Pastoral Care*, Harlow: Longman.

Wolkind, S. (1993) 'The 1989 Children Act: a cynical view from an ivory tower', *Association for Child Psychology and Psychiatry Newsletter*, 15, 40–41.

Woods, P. (1990) *Teacher Skills and Strategies*, London: Falmer Press.

Yule, W. (1989) 'The effects of disaster on children', *Newsletter, Association for Child Psychology and Psychiatry*, 11 (8) (November).

Yule, W. and Gold, A. (1993) *Wise Before The Event*, New York: Calouste Gulbenkian Foundation.

Index